IN DEFENSE OF
ghosts

BY
HERBERT B. GREENHOUSE

AN ESSANDESS SPECIAL EDITION • NEW YORK

ACKNOWLEDGMENT

The story of Nick Yelchick is from
*The Telltale Lilac Bush
and Other West Virginia Ghost Tales,*
by Ruth Ann Musick,
copyright 1965 by
The University of Kentucky Press.
Used by permission of the publishers.

IN DEFENSE OF GHOSTS

SBN: 671–10399–7

PUBLISHED BY ESSANDESS SPECIAL EDITIONS,
A DIVISION OF SIMON & SCHUSTER, INC.,
630 FIFTH AVENUE, NEW YORK, N.Y. 10020.

PRINTED IN THE U.S.A.

SECOND PRINTING

This book is dedicated
to all the nice ghosts in the world
or slightly out of it,
with the hope that the living
will receive them more graciously
into their homes.

PREFACE

Ghosts do exist. Since ancient times they have appeared to thousands of persons, young and old. They have been seen, heard, felt, and sensed. Sometimes they have come by night, often by day, even walking casually down the street in bright sunlight. They have been seen everywhere, in every country in the world, in houses old and new. They have been carefully investigated by such notable ghost-hunters as Elliott O'Donnell and Harry Price, and by researchers from the American and British Societies for Psychical Research.

No, we cannot lightly dismiss ghosts as tricks of the mind. The problem is that most people are afraid of ghosts and look upon them as enemies rather than friends. Ghosts, these people contend, are evil entities and their behavior is antisocial. They make weird noises in the night, they sneak up on mortals and frighten them out of their wits, they throw objects around a room. Most books about ghosts make matters worse by concentrating on the scary kind.

There are such spirits, it is true, but most of them are not really mean; they need help and should be treated with sympathy. When haunted mortals are tactful with their ghostly visitors, the latter often become cooperative, even friendly. A London gentleman, for example, invited a troublesome ghost to be his guest and haunt the house for as long as he liked. Thereafter, the behavior of the ghost was exemplary and when the man moved to another house, the ghost wanted to come along. In other cases, too, a sympathetic response calmed down a nervous ghost and started a friendship between living person and disembodied spirit.

Even disturbed spirits, however, do not make up the majority. There are many ghosts whose only motive is to enjoy the company of the living, apparently normal ghosts without a traumatic past. There are ghosts who come back for a cosy visit with relatives, ghosts who seek out former lovers, ghosts who drop in for a chat or at least silent communion with old friends. There are fun-loving ghosts such as the Bell Witch and the ghost of Cideville Parsonage in this book who entertain their host-families. There are domesticated ghosts who help out by washing dishes and running errands. There are literary ghosts, musical ghosts, theatrical ghosts—all of them friendly and companionable, the same personalities in spirit that they were in life.

Most ghosts want to be friendly, but their problem is one of communication. It is difficult enough for living persons to get through to each other. A spirit, lacking a physical body and the organs of speech and hearing, must learn a completely new kind of language to make mortals understand him. It is small wonder, then, that the behavior of ghosts is misunderstood, and it must be very discouraging for them when they are trying so hard to make contact with the living.

It is time the ghost had his day in court. This book argues that most ghosts are gentle, friendly, affectionate, helpful, and humorous, and submits what I believe is impressive evidence to support this claim. If there are a few nasty ghosts, the percentage is no higher than among living persons.

In the course of tracking down the pleasanter variety of ghost, I discovered some delightful ones, along with some engaging mortals who confronted them. I have no special favorite, but I was charmed by the ghost of the curé who came back searching for his snuffbox and by the gallant Gaspar, who proved such an interesting, if invisible, ghost guest. I was amused by the Vicar of Ratherby, who was upset by the apparition in the violet dress, and I applauded the courage of Athenodorus, who refused to be intimidated by the ghost with the clanking chains. And what other ghost could top Christopher Monig, the apothecary's dead apprentice, who minded the store while the owner was ill in bed?

The ghost in each of these stories is a real ghost, and in every case was seen by at least one reliable witness. In some cases many persons saw the same ghost, often at the same time, and gave depositions to investigators. Some of the stories have been embellished by legend, as in the case of the Bell Witch of Tennessee, but the original facts are still on record.

I am grateful to the following organizations for the use of their library and research facilities: The American Society for Psychical Research and the Parapsychology Foundation in New York City; the Institute for Parapsychology in Durham, North Carolina; Columbia University; Washington University in St. Louis; Duke University; and the New School for Social Research. Thanks are due to helpful librarians in several eastern, southern, and midwestern states, and to the British Society for Psychical Research for the abundant material in its publications.

H.B.G.

CONTENTS

I

AFFECTIONATE FAMILY GHOSTS

Suppose you have just died and become a spirit. You can observe your grieving relatives, but they cannot see you. You want to communicate with them, to let them know that you still live and that your love and affection for them still go on. Without a physical body and the sensory channels that make living persons comfortable with each other, you find it difficult to make your presence known. But somehow you manage to create an image of yourself or to speak to them. What happens? Chances are they will run screaming from the house.

When a ghost drops in to see his family, he wants it to be a casual, friendly visit, no different from that of living relatives. Unfortunately, many persons, even while mourning the passing of loved ones, believe that the break is complete, or if it is not, that visitors from the next world are non-human creatures in the same category with demons and other people-scaring entities. When the ghost of Mary Goffe came back to see her children, an incident described in this chapter, she must have been saddened to hear the nurse ask her in a shaking voice what manner of being she was.

Family ghosts are very patient, however, and in many cases they do gain acceptance. Some ghosts will wait many years before materializing, either because it takes them that long to master the technique of communication, or because their relatives are not ready for them. In one case, a little girl whose mother died when she was three years old saw her mother's spirit for the first time five years later. The mother kept visiting the girl and talking with her while she was growing up, giving her the same kind of help and advice a living mother would give. When the girl was twenty-one, the mother stopped her visits.

Spirits want not only to be seen and heard but also touched. Often they show their affection by kissing or embracing members of their families, and this action may help to identify them. Camille Flammarion, the astronomer who investigated ghosts, tells about a merchant marine who died several thousand miles away from the home of his favorite niece. At the time of his death, the girl was in her bedroom dressing for dinner, when she felt a hand stroking her head. She thought at first it was her mother, but no one else was in the room. When she was a child, her uncle had often taken her in his lap and stroked her hair in the same way. It was later learned that, when he died, the last word he said was her name.

In another case, investigated by the Society for Psychical Research, a man in Texas saw the ghost of his father, who was living in California. The father gave him a firm handshake, then disappeared. A moment later a telegram arrived saying that the older man had died that evening. And there is, of course, the story of Grandpa Bull, who kept his eye on his flock and expressed his affection for his wife by placing his hand on her forehead.

A DYING MOTHER
TAKES A TRIP

It is tragic when a young mother dies and leaves small children behind. It is even more poignant when for some reason she has been separated from them and fears, as she lies on her deathbed, that she will never see them again. Then a miracle often occurs—she travels in the spirit to say goodbye to her children and seems to know as she dies that she has been with them again.

One of the best-authenticated stories of this kind is that of Mary Goffe, who lived in the 17th century. Mary, a young mother of two children, came down with a serious illness, and it was thought best to send her to her father's home at West Mulling in England, nine miles from her family in Rochester. A distance of nine miles does not seem very far, but to a young woman dying in her bedroom, it might as well be halfway around the world.

Mary's children were left in the care of a nurse. The day before she died, Mary pleaded with John Goffe, her husband, to "hire a horse for I must go home and die with my children." This was impossible, of course, for she was too weak to get out of bed. That night a minister was called to her bedside. As he bent over her, she said in a voice barely above a whisper, "It is my misery that I cannot see my children."

After the minister left, a woman sat through the night at Mary's bedside. At 1 A.M. her breathing became more labored, then seemed to stop as she closed her eyes. In Rochester, at the same time, the children's nurse heard the rustle of a gown and woke up. She saw Mary coming out of the next room, where her oldest child was sleeping. Mary walked up to the nurse's bed and looked down at her youngest child, who was asleep there. Her eyes moved but she said nothing.

The nurse, now fully awake, watched her. Finally, as the bridge clock struck two, the nurse said, "In the name of the Father, Son, and Holy Ghost, what art thou?" The ghost of Mary then started to walk away. The nurse followed, but Mary vanished.

The woman at Mary's bedside noticed that she started to breathe again. The next morning just before she died Mary woke up and said, "I was with my children last night when I was asleep."

What is impressive about this story is that, although it happened in 1691, there were many witnesses and the facts were carefully checked. The morning Mary died the nurse told the story of her visit to a neighbor, Mrs. Sweet. That day Mrs. Sweet went to West Mulling, where Mary's mother told her that Mary had been to see the children. The case was investigated soon after Mary's death by the Rev. Thomas Tilson, who interviewed Mary's mother and father, the nurse, two neighbors, the minister, and the woman who had sat with her through the night.

The story of Mary Goffe was first published in Baxter's *Certainty of the World of Spirits*. In the centuries that followed there have been many such instances of affectionate mothers who travelled many miles in the spirit to see their children at the time of death or after death.

A GHOST KNOCKS
ON THE DOOR

The General lay dying in the bedroom upstairs. Little Alexandre, four years old, didn't know what "dying" meant but he knew there was something the matter with his father, and he was deeply disturbed. He adored the General, who had often taken his little son on his knee and shown him his guns and swords.

Now the lady was in the house, looking very solemn, and she took Alexandre's hand and went with him to his uncle's home a short distance away. They put him in the extra bed in his cousin Marianne's room. "Go to sleep, Alexandre," they told him. "Go to sleep, little one." But he could not sleep.

At midnight there was a loud knock on the door. His cousin Marianne, sleeping in the big bed, sat up, fear on her face. How could anyone get into the house and knock on this door when there were two outside doors that were locked? Alexandre jumped out of bed and ran to the door.

"Where are you going?" Marianne asked sharply.

"You see very well," said the child, "that I am going to open the door for Papa, who's coming to say goodbye to us."

The frightened girl forced the child back into bed, but he struggled fiercely, shouting at the top of his voice, "Goodbye, Papa! Goodbye, Papa!" Then, something like a strong masculine breath passed over his face. He went back to sleep sobbing and thinking of his father.

In the morning they told him that the General had

died just at midnight, when the knock had come. What was death? Where did his father go?

"It's all right," they said gently. "God has taken him away."

"Where does this God live?"

"He lives in the sky."

Consumed with anger, the child ran home, found a pistol in his father's collection, and hurried up the stairs. His weeping mother came out of her room and asked, "Where are you going, Alexandre?"

"I am going to the sky."

"And what will you do in the sky, my poor child?"

"I'm going to kill God, who killed Papa."

Alexandre Dumas, who gave us the dashing characters of *The Three Musketeers* and other novels, wrote this true story about himself and the ghost of his father in his *Memoirs*. As a grown man, he believed that God was on his side and not against him, and he was firmly convinced that his affectionate father had come to say goodbye on the night he left his body.

GRANDPA BULL WATCHES OVER HIS FLOCK

Samuel Bull had worked hard all his life to provide for his wife and children, but luck was against him. His salary as a London chimney sweep was so small that he couldn't even afford repairs on his ramshackle cottage, and the authorities had closed off some of the rooms as unsafe. As Sam grew older the coal dust settled in his lungs. Finally, he died of cancer, and at a very bad time, because his wife Jane was lying helpless in bed with no money and no one to care for her.

Mr. Bull's daughter moved into the cottage with her husband and five children, but it was far too crowded and the living was miserable. They made the best of it, however, and went on relief because there were too many mouths to feed. The government officials promised that they would be moved to more comfortable quarters, possibly a district council house, but nothing happened. Meanwhile, poor old Jane Bull stayed in her bedroom, thinking about Sam.

As a ghost, Grandpa Bull must have realized that he might scare the children, so he took it easy at first, walking outside their door at night to get them used to the idea. Then he let them see him go up the stairs and fade into the room where he had died. This room had been declared unsafe for living persons but was evidently all right for ghosts.

At first the children were frightened, but they gradually came to accept their ghost grandpa. Samuel Bull now appeared more often until every member of the family had seen him, sometimes when they were alone and many times when they were sitting together in the living room. After awhile they could usually tell about half an hour in advance when he was coming, and they looked forward to his visit as they would have to that of any beloved relative.

It was as though he hadn't died. He was as distinct in appearance and as solid as a living person, and he didn't glide and float like other ghosts but walked upright as he had when alive. The ghost of Grandpa Bull never appeared in his workclothes but always wore his best coat and shirt as he used to do in the evening when he came home from the chimneys. But the family could still see the poor hands of a laborer, for the knuckles seemed to come right through the skin. As a ghost Grandpa Bull wasn't as happy as he had been before he died. Something was troubling him.

The ghost reserved his tenderest affection for old Jane. He always came to her bedside and stood for long periods of time just looking at her. Twice he put his hand on her forehead, and once he called her by name. But he visited the other members of the family, too, and they reported that he sometimes stayed for several hours.

The case of Samuel Bull was investigated in 1932 by the London Society for Psychical Research. It is one of the most remarkable ghost stories on record because of the lifelike appearance of the ghost, the length of time he would stay each visit, and the fact that he was seen by every member of the family and felt by one.

Why did Grandpa Bull come back? Affection for his bedridden widow and the children was one motive. The other might have been concern for their health and comfort and a desire to prod the authorities into giving them better living conditions. The spirit of Samuel Bull became noticeably more cheerful when it was learned that the family was going to move into a local district council house. After they left the old cottage, he didn't show up any more.

II

LIVELY GHOST WIVES

Ghost wives are a special case in the family situation. As all men know, women sometimes express their love in strange ways, and this carries over into the spirit realm. The affection they feel for the husbands they have left behind is often tempered by a need for domination and control—always, the ghost wife might argue, in the best interests of the surviving spouse. Many a henpecked husband who thought he had gained his freedom discovered instead that his ghost mate had merely found new ways to keep him on his toes.

Take the matter of poker games. There was the wife of an inveterate poker player, for example, who, when she was alive, continually objected to his card games. He paid no attention, however, and at the usual hour just after dinner was off to an all-night session of beer and poker. When his wife was suddenly carried off by an infection, her husband and his pals thought this was the end of her carping, but they were mistaken. The ghost wife visited each of the men as they slept, woke them up, and told them they had better stop playing or else. One by one they dropped out of the game. Was this wife an affectionate ghost? She might think so, but there would be room for debate.

Ghost women seem to take a special delight in breaking up poker games, whether or not their husbands are involved. There was the "Lady in Black" on George's Island, off the coast of Massachusetts, who used to drop in at the most inconvenient times to taunt the soldiers at Fort Warren. This ghost, however, was irritated not with her husband, whom she tried to rescue from imprisonment during the Civil War, but with the Union soldiers who were responsible for hanging her. She got her revenge on a later generation of soldiers by rolling a stone up and down the floor every time the evening poker game started in the ordnance storeroom. The unnerved men finally gave up playing.

Not all ghost women use their powers just to pick on men, and there are several heartwarming stories about spirits who come back to help their husbands with a problem or just to show their continuing love and affection. Two stories in this chapter illustrate this kind of ghost wife. In one, the wife of a West Virginia coal miner intervenes as a ghost to save her husband's life. In the other, the dead wife of a minister proves to him through clairvoyance that she is still living in the spirit.

Ghost wives must have enjoyed themselves thoroughly in ancient times because they were given special treatment by their spouses. The custom at death was to burn their most fashionable dresses and shoes on the funeral pyre so that they would have a decent wardrobe in the next world, and they would sometimes return and give their careless husbands a tongue-lashing if their good clothes were left behind. Periander's forgetfulness caused him no end of trouble, as we shall learn later in this chapter. In another case, a golden slipper was put on the pyre but its mate left in the closet, and the irate ghost wife told her husband in no uncertain terms that it was very embarrassing for her in the spirit world. He forthwith found the slipper and had it burned.

POWER OF A WOMAN GHOST

If that old salt, Sam Blood, complained that his ghost wife was going out of her way to annoy him, he had no one to blame but himself, considering how he had treated her and the children when she was alive. Sam was a real spender, very free with his money except where his ailing wife and scrawny children were concerned. After each run with his brig to the coastal towns on the Atlantic, Sam would come back to his home port in New England and toast the boys at the Mariners' Club, where a feast would be waiting on the tavern table. The seafaring men all loved their food and liquor, but they admitted that Sam was the champ when it came to hearty eating and drinking.

Meanwhile, back at Sam's farm two miles inland, the situation was downright depressing. Since Sam rarely showed up at the farm, it was in a state of dilapidation. Sam's mother was old and feeble, his children were undernourished, and Elvira, his wife, suffered constantly from colds and other debilitating illnesses. Mrs. Blood lay in bed most of the day and moaned about the money that was going for beer and victuals to fill Sam's stomach while his family was neglected.

In spite of her weakened condition, however, Elvira was a woman of enterprise. She bided her time until one night when a big celebration was held at the Mariners' Club. On this night the round table was piled high with the most delectable foods imaginable—thick, juicy meats, puddings filled with all kinds of goodies, and scrumptious pies —strawberry, mince, apple, and peach. Along with the edibles there were bottles upon bottles of beer, wine, and liquor. Sitting in the middle of the table was a huge vat of soup, whose lovely aroma the men could sniff as they were finishing their warmup drinks in the taproom. The table almost sagged under this weight, but it was a large, sturdy affair, built of the best woods from New England forests.

Smacking their lips in anticipation, the mariners were about to sit down and enjoy their sumptuous meal when disaster struck. There was a loud crash as the table went over on its side, its precious cargo lying on the floor in a gooey mess, while the soup and drinks ran off in all directions, even invading the taproom. The men stared in horror, then roared angrily and took off after a slightly built sailor who had run out of the tavern and into the snow. They soon caught up with the culprit, seized him with rough hands, and then saw that it was Mrs. Blood disguised as a man. Without a word, Sam got out his purse and emptied its contents in payment for the ruined dinner.

No one knew why Sam took his wife with him on his

next voyage, a long trip to Savannah, Georgia. He decided to continue on to South America, saying that perhaps the trip would help Elvira regain her health. But when Sam came back, he was alone. Mrs. Blood had died, and her body had been buried at sea near Jamaica. The other men expressed their regrets to Sam, and for a few days there was no drinking and gorging at the Mariners' Club.

Having paid their respects, the men then resumed their merrymaking with even greater self-indulgence than before, Sam leading all the rest in gluttony. Now, with the spoilsport wife out of the way, another night of feasting and drinking was planned. Once more the cook worked overtime, giving special care to a succulent roast pig that was to be the main dish. Once again the men started their round of drinking in the taproom and came out with their mouths watering as they eyed the rich fare on the table.

Suddenly there was a scream, then another crash as the table lurched over on its side, and the flabbergasted men gaped at the sickening sight on the floor. The roast pig bounced in the sawdust and came to rest some distance away, a reproachful look in its eyes. The men ran around the tavern and then outside, mad with frustration as they searched for whoever was to blame, but this time they could find no villain. It was clear that no living person had overturned the table.

The following week another banquet was prepared, and again the table went over on its side. At this, the cook threw down his apron and said he had had it. He wasn't going to work all day and all night in the hot kitchen only to see his fine dishes end up on the floor. The men were inclined to sympathize with him, but they were not about to give up. Another cook was hired and another meal prepared.

The same thing happened.

Now the exasperated landlord nailed the legs of the table to the floor, but it didn't make any difference. Each time the table went up and over, and the ruined meal lay on the floor. Guards were set to watch the table day and night, but the invisible ghost of Elvira (for that was whom the men now suspected) continued to do her dirty work. Finally, the members of the Mariners' Club admitted defeat—no more dinners. They somehow felt that Sam Blood was to blame and he was given the cold shoulder from then on. Eventually the club disintegrated.

Perhaps one could say that the ghost of Mrs. Blood acted in an unfriendly way toward her husband and the other revelers. But who could blame her? It was a matter of weighing the discomfort of the undeserving against the needs of Sam's old mother and the neglected children. Alice Earle Moore, who wrote about Sam Blood and his ghost wife in *Stage-Coach and Tavern Days,* doesn't tell us if Sam finally took the hint and became a good father to his children. If not, many another meal must have been upset when he sat down at the table to eat.

THE FRIENDLY FACE
ON THE WALL

This story is much more pleasant to relate because it is about a ghost wife who had also been ill-treated when she was alive, yet she not only forgave her husband but saved his life. He, in turn, moved by her concern for him, repented and thereafter lived an exemplary life. Here is the story of Nick Yelchick, a coal miner in Grant Town, West Virginia, as told by Ruth Ann Musick in her book about West Virginia ghosts, *The Telltale Lilac Bush:*

"In March, 1927, after five years of service with the railroad, Nick Yelchick was laid off. Unable to find a job, Nick decided to forget his troubles with a bottle. When he came home drunk, he would beat his wife and tear up the house. This went on for several months.

"Finally, Nick was given a job in the mines. On Friday, after he had been working for five days, Nick asked his buddy at lunch to punch his timecard after work so he could go to the liquor store before it closed.

"As soon as Nick finished his lunch, he decided to have a look around some of the worked-out sections of the mine. Before he realized it, he was lost. The more he tried to get back to the main line, the deeper he went. He walked for four hours before he realized that nobody was going to be looking for him because his timecard would be punched out, and there would be no way of knowing that he was still in the mine. His wife would think that he had gone on one of his weekend drunks.

"About ten hours later his light burned out. Now he was really in trouble. He stumbled around for about two hours longer; then, too tired to take another step, he sat down and fell asleep. While he was sleeping, he dreamed he saw his wife's face on the wall of the mine, and she kept saying, 'Follow me.' This frightened him so much that he woke up. Just as in the dream, he saw his wife's face on the wall, so he started in the direction of the face. As soon as he got near it, another one would appear farther away. This went on for about two hours until he finally found himself on the main line. Now he was safe.

"When he got out of the mine, the night watchman said, 'Your wife was down here yesterday, looking for you, but we told her you'd gone home.'

"When Nick got home, he found his wife had killed herself. In a note she said, 'I thought you would stop drinking when you got this job, but now I know different.'

"After that, Nick became a model citizen of Grant Town and was until his death in 1947."

A GHOST WIFE
WHO PASSED
THE TEST

The ghost wife in this story was neither heavy-handed, like Mrs. Blood, nor—like Nick's wife—bent on returning good for evil. She was merely a gay, cheerful spirit who was delighted with her ghostly powers and wanted to show them off for her husband. Even more important is that she wanted to convince him that she still lived and still loved him.

The husband was a well-known Philadelphia minister, the Rev. Russell H. Conwell, at one time president of Temple University. The Rev. Conwell told about his experience to Bruce Barton in an interview published in the *American Magazine* of July, 1921. The story also appeared in several newspapers.

Each morning, said the Rev. Conwell, the ghost of his dead wife would appear in a dream at the foot of the bed. She would be smiling and looking roguish. He didn't think she was real, however, and told her so. She insisted that she was the spirit of his wife. All right, then, he said, would she submit to a test? Smiling, she agreed.

The following morning, when she was there again at the foot of his bed, he put a question to her. Where was his army discharge paper? He had not seen it for a number of years and had no idea where it might be. She promptly answered that it was in a black box behind some books in the library. He got out of bed and went into the library where, sure enough, he found the paper in a box behind some books on a shelf.

The next morning she appeared again, smiling slyly, and said, "Now will you believe?" The Rev. Conwell said he still wasn't convinced and asked if he could test her again. She agreed. She was quite sure of her powers.

At breakfast that morning the Rev. Conwell told his maid that a gold fountain pen his wife had given him some years before was lying on his desk. Would she take it off the desk and hide it, not telling him or anyone else what hiding place she had chosen?

The ghost of Mrs. Conwell appeared on schedule the following morning, sitting at the foot of the bed and wearing a bright smile. In reply to his question, she said of course she knew where the fountain pen was hidden.

"Come with me," she said gaily. He got out of bed and she took his hand, or at least he felt something like her hand in his. She led him to a closet, in which the top shelf had been converted into a small compartment with a door. She pointed to this compartment. He stood on a chair and, stretching his hand in behind the small door, pulled out the pen.

The Rev. Conwell was now convinced that it was really his wife who had appeared to him so many mornings and cheerfully demonstrated how a ghost wife could come alive.

THE GHOST QUEEN
WHO NEEDED
A NEW DRESS

In ancient times it was thought that ghosts acquired wisdom they may not have had while alive. Rulers who had agonizing decisions to make and did not trust their advisors often summoned spirits, when they were available, and asked them what to do.

Wives who had been ignored by their husbands during their lifetimes were held in higher esteem as ghosts. One ruler who kept asking the spirit of his wife for advice was Periander of Corinth and, according to the Greek historian Herodotus, she made the most of it. Periander, who was known as the Tyrant of Corinth, had had her put to death one day when he was in a bad mood, and as a ghost she was in no hurry to give service.

Ghosts are very good at finding lost objects, and when Periander mislaid a valuable article a friend had left with him for safekeeping, he asked the oracle at Thesprotia to call up his dead wife's spirit. She took her time about materializing, and when Periander asked her where the object was, she remained silent.

"Speak, woman!" cried the exasperated Periander. "I must find the treasure before my friend returns. Speak, I beseech you."

The ghost, whose name was Melissa, replied that she was not suitably dressed for a consultation—in fact, she wasn't even dressed. When Periander had had her executed, he had disposed of her wardrobe but neglected to follow the custom of having her clothes burned on the funeral pyre, and now she had to go around the spirit world without any clothes on. Not only was she cold, but it was humiliating for one of her position. Before she could meet with him, he would have to get her garments appropriate to her status as the dead wife of a ruler.

Where, asked Periander plaintively, could he find her such garments? At this, she merely smiled enigmatically, as wives often do, and told him that was his problem. Then she vanished.

Now this Periander was not only a strong ruler but a resourceful one. The women of Corinth, he noted, were always luxuriously dressed in gowns of rich cloth with jeweled decorations. He bided his time until a festival day approached. Then, when all the women were assembled in the agora (town square), resplendent in their best holiday apparel, he mounted the podium to make a welcoming speech. The next moment a gasp went through the crowd.

Periander told the women to take off their clothes.

Today, no king or other head of government would dare order a mass striptease when the ladies of a community are gathered in public, but in those days it could be done. Periander explained that he needed the clothes to burn in a huge fire in his wife's honor. The women could not refuse this kind of request, and there, in the shadow of the temple of Apollo, they reluctantly took off their beautiful gowns and threw them into the fire.

Later Melissa appeared to Periander again, looking every inch the ghost queen in her dazzling finery, a pleased smile on her face. She embraced her husband and thanked him, then told him where to find the lost object.

The historian leaves us dissatisfied on several points. For example, although Periander found the lost article where the ghost queen said it would be, we do not learn if her advice was equally good on later occasions. As to the reactions of the husbands whose wives were ordered to take off their clothes, Herodotus is discreetly silent.

[III]

GHOSTLY FRIENDS
AND LOVERS

The love and concern of a ghost are not limited to just his family. There are many accounts of warm friendships that seem to continue after one of the friends dies, not only in the memory of the one still alive but also in the soul of the returning spirit. There are stories, too, about love affairs that continue after death, although there is a certain sadness about most of these stories because of the obstacles to the love.

In some cases, friends make an agreement while still alive that the first to die will contact the other one. Lord Brougham, a writer and statesman of the early 19th century, made such a pact with a friend, written in their own blood, while both were students at the University of Edinburgh. Years later, while Lord Brougham was lying in his bath one evening, he saw the ghost of his friend in a nearby chair, looking at him. Word came later that the friend had died in India. In another case, the wife of a minister had made a pact with a schoolgirl friend, but the friend's spirit appeared not to the wife but to the minister. When he told his wife that the ghost had had an unusually elegant hairdo, she replied that her friend had always spent a great deal of time fixing her hair.

Many ghosts return because of an unhappy love affair, either to seek the object of their affections or to wander about the places that hold memories of their lost loves. In her book *Among the Isles of Shoals*, Celia Thaxter writes about a ghostly young lady wearing a dark seacloak who stands on a hill of a lonely island off the coast of New England and waits for the return of her pirate lover. She keeps repeating in a mournful voice, "He will come again. He *will* come again." There are also ghostly lovers such as the gentle Evelyn Byrd who seem forever attached to the homes where they lived through their sorrows.

There are many ghost stories about love affairs between living persons and spirits they did not know in the flesh. Hereward Carrington tells about an artist friend who was visited by a winsome young girl ghost who encouraged him in his work and came often to look at his paintings. Another story is about the sensitive poet Ernest Dowson, who saw a beautiful girl ghost at the home of a friend and later met a young lady who was her exact image. The story loses credibility, however, when the very live and warm-blooded girl suddenly becomes a ghost herself without going through the usual procedure of dying.

A GHOST LOVER
ON HORSEBACK

Her name was Charity and she lived in a cabin in the Carolinas. She was a simple girl, warmhearted and constant in her affections, as most girls were in those days. When she loved a man, it was for all time—for her whole life and later, if there was another life. When handsome Henry Galbreath wooed her, she could not resist him. He was a fine figure of a young man, tall, straight, and strong. And what a thrill to see him on his horse, galloping each day down the river road that led to her cabin!

One day Henry told her they could not marry until the British had been driven back across the sea. He had enlisted in the Continental Army and would be gone for one year. At the end of the year he would return and they would be married—if he were still alive. If he were dead, he would still come back to her, he vowed, and would be riding on his horse down the river road.

A year went by and the British were defeated. But there had been no word from Henry in all that time. Then the day came when he had promised he would return. All day she watched from the door of her cabin, peering anxiously down the river road. No one came that day, either by foot or on horseback. The sun went down and a storm broke. Charity went inside and sat at the kitchen table, listening. But all she could hear that summer evening was the sound of the rain as it beat down on the roof of her cabin.

She finally undressed slowly and got into bed, but her eyes stayed open as she thought of her absent lover. Had he died in battle? But he had promised to return, dead or alive. Did the dead return? Henry had said they did, and he could not be wrong.

Then, in the middle of the night, she heard a faint sound in the distance—the far-off gallop of horses' hoofs, getting louder and louder. Her heart beating wildly, she quickly dressed and ran to the door just as the horse stopped in front of it.

She opened the door and saw him sitting there, in a circle of light, a flowing robe around his shoulders. They looked at each other, but her heart was so full she could not speak. Then horse and rider wheeled around and galloped down the road, becoming smaller and smaller. And as she watched, the light died away against the dark clouds, and they vanished.

The next day Charity walked up and down the river road, looking for some sign of Henry's visit the night before. But even in the soft mud there were no hoofprints. Yet he came again that night on his horse, and the night after that, and each time he just looked at her and rode away in a pool of light. And then one night he didn't come, and she never saw him again.

Girls were faithful in those days, even after the deaths of their lovers. Charity stayed in her cabin the rest of her life. She never married but lived with the memory of her ghostly lover on his galloping horse.

The story of Charity is no tale spun out of the imagination of the folks in South Carolina. Her full name was Charity Miles, she lived with her seventy-year-old father, and she was only eighteen when she met Henry Galbreath. Her neighbors and friends told their children and grandchildren about her, and the case was finally reported in a newspaper during the 1860s.

THE GENTLE GHOST OF EVELYN BYRD

If there is one lesson the history of ghosts can teach a father, it is that his daughter is sure to come back as a spirit and haunt the ancestral home if she is not allowed to marry her lover. An example is the ghost of Eloise DeSaussure, who was put into a French convent by her father because she wanted to marry a Huguenot. She lived back in the 16th century, but she is still getting even with her father by haunting a house in Camden, South Carolina, owned by a descendant of the DeSaussure family.

An even more famous case is that of Evelyn Byrd, the Westover ghost of Virginia. The Westover plantation belonged to Col. William Byrd II and was built in the early 1700s. The Colonel often took his daughter over to London, and on one occasion she fell in love with Charles Mordaunt, son of the Earl of Petersborough. Since Charles was a Catholic and the Byrds were Protestants, the Colonel objected to her romance and whisked the girl back to America on the next boat.

For the beautiful, gentle Evelyn, one love affair in a lifetime was enough. She stayed close to the Westover mansion, rejecting the suitors who stood in line to ask for her hand. Still in her twenties, she had the firm conviction she would die before she was thirty, and she confided to a friend that she would reappear as a spirit. Sure enough, following her death at twenty-eight, the friend saw her standing beside her grave, in a white dress. The ghost smiled at her friend and blew a kiss, then faded away.

The ghost of Evelyn is still seen, drifting ethereally about the garden and grounds at Westover. As in life, she is a gentle, delicate wraith, appearing silently to the guests who visit Westover, alway smiling and blowing kisses.

Those who have seen the ghost describe her as floating a little above the ground.

As long as Westover stands, Evelyn will not leave it. She seems determined to let her father know, wherever he is, that he made a bad mistake when he kept her from marrying Charles Mordaunt.

THE GRATEFUL GHOST

A very touching story about a friendly ghost was told in a letter written by Dr. Cabral, a physician from Brazil. Dr. Cabral had taken a poor orphan named Déolinda into his home, fed and clothed her, and shown her kindness she had not previously known in her brief life. While still a young girl, Déolinda contracted tuberculosis and died.

A year later Dr. Cabral went to live in the house of a friend, Monsieur Barbosa de Andrade, where he continued his medical practice. During this time de Andrade's sister was taken ill, and Dr. Cabral would look in each evening after his rounds to see how she was. One night, exhausted from the day's work, Dr. Cabral went to sleep in his room, while the girl's two sisters stayed with the patient in her room.

During the night he felt the pressure of a soft hand upon his cheek and woke up. No one was in the room. The next moment the invisible hand was pressed against his head. "I had the sensation," he wrote, "that someone was holding my head and placing something around it."

Dr. Cabral called to the girls in the next room. One of them, Felicia, who had demonstrated psychic powers, said, "I see at your bedside a spirit child clothed in white. She places on your head a crown of roses. She says her name is Déolinda, and she has come to show her gratitude for the generosity you showed in taking care of her."

Dr. Cabral felt the crown of roses on his head and the touch of the girl's hand, but he could not see or hear

Déolinda. As he lay in bed thinking about her, he suddenly remembered that this night marked the anniversary of her death. He had not thought of her for some time and had never mentioned her to anyone in the house.

Dr. Cabral's letter was sent in 1892, and the case was published in 1894 by the Society for Psychical Research.

FIVE FINGER EXERCISE

Once in a while, a friendship develops between a young boy and an older man, and it can be a rich experience for both. Edward, only fourteen, knew that his French tutor had little money and was in poor health, but the boy was touched because for him Monsieur La Tappy always put on a cheerful face. Edward sensed the deep sadness within the old man, who expressed it this way: "Pour moi il n'y a pas de dieu." God might exist for others, but not for Monsieur La Tappy.

Still, he wasn't really old. He was only fifty, but he looked older because he was so small and thin and there were such deep hollows in his cheeks. Threads showed everywhere in his coat, and he was always cold, always blowing on his swollen fingers as he walked in the never-ending London rain. It was sad, too, about those fingers because Monsieur La Tappy taught piano as well as French, and a chronic case of chilblains kept his fingers stiff. Often, while he was discussing literature or painting with Edward, he would work his fingers in the air to make them limber, saying with a laugh, "Je joue mon piano."

Edward had rented a room off the Golden Square in London and was studying painting at Heatherly's. It was a quaint section of town where he lived, very musical, with street-singers filling the air with song all day. Edward went to art school every day from nine to four, then hurried back to his room for his French lesson. Monsieur La Tappy was always there at the stroke of four, and Edward would put the kettle on to boil for tea. He knew that his French tutor did not get enough to eat, but La Tappy was a proud man and would refuse any offer of a meal. Tea, yes, but no food.

After the lesson and a leisurely discussion of drama and other worthwhile subjects, La Tappy would leave, swinging his umbrella jauntily as though he hadn't a care in the world. But when Edward looked out the window a few moments later, he would see the little figure hunched under the umbrella, walking dejectedly to his next lesson because he could not afford bus fare.

One day the rain came down harder than ever, and Edward was late from school. He rushed upstairs to his room because he did not want to keep La Tappy waiting, but when he opened the door and looked inside, no one was there. As he was putting the kettle on the stove, he had a strange feeling. He looked up and saw La Tappy standing with his back to the window. The young man shivered but didn't know why.

La Tappy seemed quieter, more pensive than usual. Edward took his coat, made a fire, and boiled tea. They had their usual French lesson, drank tea, and talked about Spain and the Alhambra Palace, but Edward felt that something was wrong. Now and then La Tappy would do his five finger exercise, working his bloated fingers in the air with his eyes closed. Today he did not even pretend to be gay.

It was 5:30, time to leave. Taking his coat and umbrella from the boy, La Tappy walked slowly to the door, then suddenly turned and stared at Edward. His face had gone chalk-white. He raised his right hand and pointed at the sky, then seemed to fade away, right through the door.

Edward stood for a moment, staring at the door, then ran to the window to watch for the reassuring figure of La Tappy fighting the rain with bowed shoulders. He waited, but no La Tappy appeared in the street below. He went back to the door and opened it. A young man was standing there.

"Monsieur Edward? I am sorry to disturb you but I bring bad news. My father, Monsieur La Tappy, could not see you at four o'clock today because he has died."

"But he was here!"

"No, monsieur. My father died suddenly at 3 P.M. And just before he died, he said one word—'Pardon.' "

This incident is described in Edward H. Sothern's *My Remembrances: The Melancholy Tale of "Me."* Sothern, who was the young art student of the story, later became a noted actor on the London stage. One of his earliest and fondest memories was of a gentle French tutor who was also his friend, who came to visit him after death and talked of many things while he did his silent five finger exercise.

GHOSTS WHO HELP WITH THE CHORES

There is one type of ghost, not always a friend or relative, who can never get enough work to do around the house. This ghost enjoys washing dishes, sweeping floors, bringing tea up to the sickroom—any kind of chore that will make it easier for the family or the servants. One motherly ghost even nursed a baby, or so the child claimed when she grew up. Ghosts have also been known to wait on customers in a store when the owner was incapacitated, as witness the famous case of Christopher Monig in the 17th century.

The only problem with the service-oriented ghost is that he often takes his duties far too seriously, and once he is on the job, he can be stopped only at the risk of injury to the mortals who get in his way. The overzealous ghost maid discussed in this chapter is an example, and it took the intervention of a king to slow her down. Another example is the Cauld Lad of Hylton, who worked an eight-hour day and overtime, washing and stacking dishes, dusting furniture, and vacuuming the rug. When all the rooms were spotless and there was nothing to do, the Cauld Lad would be furious and would make more work by spilling milk on the floor or tracking dirt into the house.

A more genial ghost was Tom, just as industrious as the Cauld Lad but not as temperamental. Tom, mentioned in Gertrude Cummins' *Unseen Adventures,* attached himself to a Mr. Cockle, the rector of Lissinford back about 1842, and made sure that the rector was freed of petty household matters so that he could attend to his parish duties. On one occasion the rector's wife put aside a ham to boil, and found the next day that Tom had boiled it. Letters that were placed on the hall table were delivered to their destination without going through the post office. Guests of the rector often saw a broom sweeping the floor, wielded by an invisible Tom, who sang hymns as he worked.

Sometimes all the owner of a haunted house has to do is ask for service and he'll get it. Flammarion tells in *Haunted Houses* about a ghost named Coco who was about as obstreperous and troublesome a spirit as could be found until he was given an assignment. Coco made the traditional ghost noises, laughed hysterically, threw books off their shelves, and frightened away the relatives of Mme. Manoel de Granford, who rented the house. Mme. de Granford wasn't intimidated. She spoke softly to the ghost and asked him to help out from time to time.

One evening, while Mme. de Granford was getting ready to go to the theatre, she told Coco she was expecting an important letter. Would Coco please rap twice on the mirror if the letter was on its way and would arrive that evening? Coco promptly gave two raps and the letter arrived as predicted.

THE GHOST WHO SERVED BREAKFAST

In the 19th century there were a number of devout ghosts who moved in with ministers and priests and took over the household chores. The Rev. Morell Theobald had so many visitations that he kept a diary and wrote a book called *Spirit Workers in the Home Circle.*

The Rev. Theobald had a live servant who was gifted with clairvoyance but was not especially industrious. Although it was her duty to have breakfast ready at 8 A.M., she was usually just turning over in bed at that time. One morning when she came down late, she discovered that the fire had already been lit and the water for tea was hot in the kettle. Mary was surprised but not unhappy that a mysterious visitor had done her job.

The next morning Mary came down late again and found the milk can sitting on the table. Getting it there would have been a problem for a human being, let alone a ghost, since it was habitually left outside the locked garden gate, and it would have had to be carried not only past the gate but also through the locked rear door. The next morning Mary was ready for anything. Sure enough, the table cover had been placed over the breakfast table, and the food was cooked and waiting.

Mary was now curious enough to get up on time and see if she could surprise the ghost in action. The following morning she took a box of matches and was about to light the fire when it lit itself. Every morning after that the fire lit itself and continued to do so for three years. Mary also found kettles that had been left empty the night before filled with water and whistling on the stove.

By this time the Rev. Theobald had accepted the reality of the spirits (he thought there were more than one) and considered them part of the family. On October 20, 1884, he wrote in his diary:

> "Upon the kitchen table a small tray was ready, with two cups and saucers upon it, to take up an early cup of tea to myself and wife, a luxury the spirits commenced some months ago when we were out of health, and have continued ever since. . . . On the table were biscuits, sugar, and milk, and a fresh sardine box ready opened for breakfast. . . ."

Although Theobald, his wife, and Mary appreciated the presence of their ghost helpers, the other members of their community held contrary views. One day a boy who came regularly to take the shoes out to be cleaned was going down the stairs and "was met by the tray coming up." A collision between the floating tray and the boy was avoided when the tray was placed on the top stair. The boy left the house in a hurry.

Other ministers, perhaps lacking such efficient maid service, denounced the Rev. Theobald from their pulpits, solemnly declaring that he had made a pact with the devil. Theobald dismissed this charge with some well-chosen words: "For if it be Satan, he is certainly domesticated and changed into an angel of light, or certainly firelight. He has exchanged his medieval tail for a 19th century apron."

The Rev. Theobald had lost three children when they were very small, and he suspected they were the helpful spirits. If so, the little ghosts were able to express their affection in practical ways as they would have done if still alive.

THE OVERZEALOUS GHOST MAID

The priest was seated in his study, waiting for the new maid to arrive. There was much work to do—the articles on the shelves would have to be rearranged, all the furniture dusted, pots and pans scrubbed, rugs cleaned. Too bad young Hilda had died so suddenly and long before her time. She had been a conscientious servant, if sometimes too forceful in the way she wielded her household utensils, and she had kept the rectory spotless. He hoped the new girl would be as efficient.

There was a knock on the door, and with a sigh the priest went to open it. The young lady standing there curtsied politely and the priest asked her in. She was a quiet little thing, modest and self-effacing, and she listened respectfully as the priest outlined her duties. Then, as he was busy with his own work, he dismissed her. A little later, looking up from the sermon he was preparing, he smiled. He could hear the water going from the tap in the kitchen and the sound of industrious hands scrubbing the pots.

A moment later there was a scream. The priest jumped

up from his desk and ran into the kitchen. The new maid was huddled in a corner, her eyes wide with terror.

"She pulled the pot right out of my hand!" exclaimed the maid. "Right out of my hand she pulled it—with such a strong tug I could not hold on to it."

"She?" inquired the priest wonderingly. He turned to the sink and stared at the pot in disbelief. It was literally scrubbing itself, and the next moment it placed itself on the drainboard, while another pot rose in the air and settled in the sink.

The priest couldn't account for this phenomenon. Pots don't wash themselves. He led the trembling girl out of the kitchen and into the chapel, put a dustrag in her hand, and told her to clean off the pews. Then he went back to his study to think about this strange occurrence.

Again there was a yell: "No, please—don't—don't!"

Hurrying into the chapel, he saw what seemed to be a tug-of-war between the new maid and something invisible that was pulling at the rag. The new girl was determined, but she was no match for the ghost of Hilda. The astonished priest saw the rag leap out of the maid's hand, quickly dust off one pew, then sail in the air and descend on the next one, dusting it off. The rag travelled from pew to pew, cleaning them in record time, then plopped on the last one and rested there. The next moment there was a rush of wind past the priest, and the fire lit up in his study. Now the furniture began sliding around the study, the priest's desk and chair included.

The new maid left that day.

For several days after that the priest did not know a moment's peace. If it was indeed the ghost of Hilda cleaning up the rectory, she was rather overdoing it. The ghost worked in a frenzy, flying from room to room as she scrubbed floors and polished the furniture. Several times the priest barely got out of the way as a mop or broom whizzed by. The ghost was determined to clean every object in the church until it shone, and too bad for any mortal who crossed her path.

The priest couldn't take it. Regretfully, for he had always liked Hilda and appreciated her coming back as a ghost and helping out, he sent word to the king, who happened to be Frederick the Great of Prussia. Frederick dispatched two officers to look into the case, but they were almost immediately sorry they had come. They arrived on a day when the ghost maid had decided to do a little redecorating, and the furniture was zigzagging around the room. No sooner would she arrange the pieces in one pattern than she decided to try another. The presence of the officers annoyed her no end, and she whacked the daylights out of them when they got in her way, which was impossible to avoid since they couldn't see her.

The officers reported to Frederick that the church was not only haunted but by as ornery a ghost as they had ever encountered. Besides, the priest could get no rest and his work was suffering. Frederick decided on the only sensible course—he had the church torn down and rebuilt elsewhere.

The overzealous ghost maid appeared in the 18th century and was first reported by ghostologist Adolphe d'Assier. I don't know if Hilda was her real name, but it will do as well as any other.

THE GHOST WHO
MINDED THE STORE

The members of the Academy of Leipzig were engaged in heated debate. The year was 1659, and the meeting had been called to decide a very serious question: Had the ghost of Christopher Monig appeared in Silesia or hadn't it? The testimony of customers who had come into the pharmacy was very convincing. They were willing to swear that Christopher's ghost had waited on them. Skeptics said, however, that either they were making up the story or they had merely imagined they had seen Christopher.

When the apothecary fell ill just after the death of his

apprentice, he tossed feverishly on his sickbed, wondering who would mind the store. Christopher, who had been a most conscientious employee during his lifetime, must have gotten the message and decided that, dead or not, he would fill in for his absent employer. When the first customer walked into the pharmacy with her prescription, she stared in horror at the ghost of Christopher standing behind the counter. Christopher said nothing, just lifted the prescription out of her paralyzed hand, disappeared into the laboratory, came back with a bottle which he handed to the lady, took her money, and put it in a drawer. She stumbled out with the bottle.

The next customer got the same kind of shock, but silently handed her prescription to the ghostly clerk, who quickly collected the pills and put them in a container which he wrapped up and handed to her. He took the money from her shaking fingers, placed it in the drawer, then nodded stiffly as she groped for the doorknob.

All day the customers came in, had their prescriptions filled, and went out into the street looking as if they had seen a ghost, which they had. Christopher nimbly handled pots and flasks as he had done when alive, arranged his bottles neatly on shelves, pounded and tasted drugs, swept the floor, and put everything in order at night when he left. The customers were understandably nervous, but they had no cause for complaint. Christopher was as efficient as ever, if a bit brusque and not inclined to conversation.

One afternoon Christopher decided he had had enough and changed from a dependable ghost into an unpredictable one. Putting on an old coat that had been hanging in the pharmacy, he left the store and walked along the street, to the consternation of shoppers who had known him in the flesh. He walked purposefully, glancing neither right nor left, then turned into a street where a friend lived, went into the house, stared silently at his petrified friend, and went out again. He visited the homes of each of his old friends, gave them a piercing stare, and left.

Finally, he wandered down to the cemetery, where he met a servant girl and for the first time, so far as anyone knew, he spoke: "Go to your master's house and dig in the lower room; you will find there an inestimable treasure." The girl, not used to ghosts, fainted, but later recalled his words and dug up the spot mentioned, finding a bloodstone.

When the apothecary had recovered and was back at work, his excited customers told him the story and advised him to burn everything in the pharmacy that had belonged to Christopher, thus assuring that the ghost would not return. It is not known whether the apothecary did so, but he should have been pleased rather than distressed with his late employee. The ghost had minded the store well in his absence and had left a nice sum of money in the drawer for him.

The evidence was overwhelming. The skeptics were voted down, and the consensus among the members of the Academy of Leipzig was that the ghost of Christopher Monig had in truth been seen in town. All the facts are on record in the annals of the Academy.

THE SPIRIT
WHO WAS AFRAID
OF FIRE

While she was alive she was a devoted wife, a solicitous mother, and a conscientious housekeeper. At intervals throughout the day she would go through every room, looking for dust to wipe off, or vigorously mop the floor to get rid of dirt and lint. She was especially afraid of fires and would keep looking anxiously at the fireplace to be sure that smoldering embers were not escaping.

Although she loved all her children, she was particularly concerned about Henry, who was not too well and who made a bare living fashioning pencils in the small back room on the second floor. She would often go into the room and clean up after Henry, because so many pieces of wood and lead would lie on the floor. You had to excuse Henry because he was trying to be a writer, and writers always had their minds elsewhere, even when they were good at making pencils.

She died, as all men and women do, but she still worried about the house. Who was living there now? Were they keeping all the rooms clean and free of dirt? Were they careful to sprinkle ashes over the coals so that fire would not break out and destroy the frame house? As a ghost she looked in one day and said something like "Oh my!" when she saw the present inhabitants.

Not that she didn't like them. They were fine people, the Alcotts, and very talented. Bronson Alcott was a very good writer (Henry had said so and there was no better judge of literary ability) and his daughter Louisa had written a famous book—*Little Women*. But writers didn't know how to keep house, and they were apt to be careless with matches. She would have to visit her old home from time to time and see that everything was in order.

The name of this motherly spirit was Mrs. Thoreau, and her son was the immortal Henry David Thoreau, writer of *Walden* and member of a distinguished literary group residing in Concord, Massachusetts, in the 19th century. Mrs. Thoreau's ghost was first seen by Mary, the Alcotts' maid, who described her accurately although she had never seen the lady in the flesh. Later Bronson, Louisa, and the rest of the family saw her, too, and of course they recognized the mother of their late friend.

She would appear first at the front door, a tall lady wearing a large white cap, her handkerchief tucked neatly into the waistband of her full skirt. She would look around the room for a moment as if trying to surprise a speck of dust, then bend down and run her finger along the edge of the baseboard. Then she would hurry to the fireplace and make movements over it with her hands, as if extinguishing escaping embers. Finally she would go up to the room where Henry had made his pencils and see that it was tidy.

To the Alcotts, a friend such as Mrs. Thoreau was always welcome, alive or dead, even though she did go fussing about and making sure everything was spic-and-span. Not so Mary. The ghost of Mrs. Thoreau made her nervous, and she once claimed that the bed stood on two legs. It never occurred to Mary that Mrs. Thoreau still felt responsible for the condition of the house where so many masterpieces had been written and wanted it to stand as long as possible as a memorial to her son Henry.

[V]

GHOSTS WHO ARE GUESTS

Many ghosts, like mothers-in-law, come for a short visit and stay on indefinitely. This is understandable when the ghost wishes to see his relatives or friends, or has a sentimental attachment to a house he once lived in that has been taken over by strangers. In the latter case, unless some dramatic event or unfinished business has called him back, all he wants to do is putter around and enjoy the scenes of his past, and he is usually careful not to disturb the present tenants.

There is one type of ghost, however, who appears in a house unfamiliar to him during his lifetime and as a complete stranger to the persons living in it. He is there simply because he enjoys their company and likes the surroundings. For the most part, these are normal spirits with no unhappy memories to plague their ghostly minds. Generally, they are cheerful and fun-loving, and they enter with zest into the daily life of each member of the household.

The adopted families of spirits, with the possible exception of the Bell family, seem to enjoy their ghosts and treat them either as members of the family or as honored guests. Some very delightful ghosts have had the status of guests. A French Huguenot ghost, who was the guest of a family in South Carolina, told fortunes and always predicted good luck. Once he said that the girl of the house would win a high-school prize, and the ghost was as proud as any member of the family when his prediction came true.

Two of the ghost guests discussed in this chapter belong to the group of spirits who "adopt" their hosts. The third, Karl Clint, is included because, although he started out as a disturbed spirit who felt that the house belonged to him rather than to the mortal who leased it, a cordial ghost–host relationship was finally worked out between them. Of the three ghosts, Gaspar was by far the most charming and Karl Clint the moodiest. The Bell Witch was undoubtedly the most versatile and clever of the three, but she could make life miserable for the family when she wanted to be mean, especially for poor John Bell.

Sometimes it is the ghost who looks upon himself as host and the living persons as guests. A family in Dover, Delaware, had just moved into a new residence when the ghost of a dignified-looking gentleman appeared in the house, bowing and smiling in welcome. This ghost thought, however, that his guests were careless with the electricity, and he would always turn off the refrigerator light after dinner, an act which so unnerved the servants that they gave notice. The lady of the house considered having the gentleman ghost exorcised by a clergyman, but didn't do it because it would be a discourtesy to such a friendly spirit.

Then there are the convivial ghosts who merely show up for an evening, have a drink or two, and go back to the spirit world. Other fun-loving ghosts return as guests to indulge in the sports and hobbies they enjoyed when alive. One ghost, mentioned in William Oliver Stevens' *Unbidden Guests,* added herself to a party of four at a bridge table. Elliott O'Donnell, in his *Rooms of Mystery,* describes a haunted house in Cardiff, Wales, where two ghosts meet from time to time and have a boxing match.

THE GHOST WITH
HIS OWN ROOM

Psychic persons are drawn either by accident or design to haunted places. Known "sensitives," such as Eileen Garrett, are often asked to step inside a house suspected of having mysterious vibrations and put their astral fingers to the wind to see if they can sense a ghostly presence. Then the parapsychologists study their reports and write learned monographs for professional journals devoted to "psi" phenomena.

Other psychics stumble upon ghosts inadvertently, as if subconsciously attracted to them. One of these was Count Louis Hamon, also known as Cheiro, who wrote books on palmistry and made predictions of world events. Hamon rented an old house in London just before World War I, a large and rambling mansion surrounded by trees and set well back from the road. Before moving in, he found out that the previous owner was leaving because he was disturbed by strange noises, but to one such as Hamon, who was familiar with the occult, the possible presence of a ghost was more of a challenge than a deterrent.

While the house was being redecorated, its only occupants were Count Hamon and his secretary, Perkins. During the first night the Count was sleeping in his ground-floor bedroom, when he heard footsteps coming up the stairs that led to the basement. The footsteps came to the door of his room, there was a pause, and then a loud knock. The Count picked up a poker from the fireplace and opened the door, but no one was there. He closed the door and waited. There was another knock—again no one at the door. Perkins came out of the adjoining room, pale with fear, and vowed he would leave at once, but Count Hamon persuaded him to remain.

The following night the two men stayed in Hamon's room and sat in armchairs facing the fire, armed with stout pokers. In the early-morning hours they heard the footsteps coming up again and stopping at their door. Then—after a brief pause—there was another loud knock and the click of a light switch outside. Cautiously, Perkins opened the door. No one was there, but the landing was flooded with light. The two men went down to the basement but found it empty. There was a room about halfway up the stairs between the basement and the first floor, but it was locked.

A few days later Hamon had a visitor, dramatist Henry Hamilton, who knew about the ghost. Friends of

Hamilton's had once lived in the house, and during a séance in the living room, the ghost had told Hamilton his story. When Hamon described what had happened, Hamilton wrote out the ghost's story and put it in a sealed envelope, which he gave to Hamon.

When the redecorating was complete, Hamon hired servants and had a housewarming party. After the meal, while the guests were seated around the fire in the living room, they heard sharp raps on a crystal bowl. Hamon addressed the invisible ghost, saying he would call out the letters of the alphabet and that the ghost should knock on the bowl each time he reached a letter that would help spell out the message.

"My name is Karl Clint," the raps spelled out. "I lived here about a hundred and twenty years ago." The ghost then said he would give no more information in the drawing room; the mortals would have to go down to the room off the basement stairway and assemble there. Hamon and his guests descended the stairway and went into the room, seating themselves around a small table with just a lighted candle in the center.

Now the ghost spelled out the messages with taps on the bare wall. His first statement was that it was *his* house; they should go away and leave him alone. Then he confessed that he had murdered a man who was trying to take his sweetheart away from him and had buried the man beneath the house. He refused to say any more.

Later that evening, Hamon opened the sealed envelope and found that it contained the same information the ghost had just given him. He checked old records of the parish and discovered that the room off the stairway had been part of a farmhouse owned in the 18th century by a man named Karl Clint. The records also mentioned the disappearance of one Arthur Liddel, whom Clint had named as the murdered man. It was further stated that the house had gradually been enlarged during the next hundred years.

When Hamon opened up many of the old rooms, the ghost of Karl Clint showed his displeasure by knocking violently on the walls. Hamon decided to hold a séance and called in a blind medium. Turning out all the lights in the drawing room, the Count and his friends sat with the medium around a table lit only by a small lamp and waited.

Suddenly there was a loud banging on the ceiling, then on the mirror and the chandelier above their heads. From below came the sound of stamping feet which stopped just outside the door of the drawing room. A shadowy mist appeared in the room, then a man materialized. He was about forty-five years old and had a close-cropped beard and red hair.

The ghost asked plaintively why all these people were in his house. Count Hamon spoke to him in a sympathetic voice and asked if he could help him in any way. All he wanted, said the ghost, was to remain in the house with Charlotte, his 18th-century love. He had never been happy anywhere but here.

Count Hamon and the ghost finally made a deal. Karl would stay with Charlotte in the room off the stairway, and it would remain locked. The mortals could live in the rest of the house, and if they did not bother the ghost and his girl friend, he would not disturb them.

For years there were no more knockings or other ghostly noises. Then, Hamon decided to move to another house in London but thought he would first say goodbye to his strange guest. He held another séance and thanked Karl for keeping his end of the bargain. Was there anything he could do for the ghost before he left?

Yes, was the surprising answer. Could he, the ghost of Karl Clint, live with Count Hamon in his new house? The Count was the only person who had ever been kind to him, and he would like to be his permanent guest. Hamon invited him to come along and bring Charlotte with him.

Count Hamon does not tell us whether he fixed up a

room in the new house for Karl and his girl friend. Since he never heard from the ghost again, the 18th-century lovers must have been satisfied with the new arrangement.

THE FUN-LOVING
BELL WITCH

One of America's enduring, though not endearing, ghosts is the hell-raising Bell Witch of Tennessee. Opinion would be divided in the Bell family as to whether the Witch was a friendly ghost. John Bell, the head of the house, would say, emphatically, no, his wife Lucy would be more charitable, while Betsy, their daughter, would probably not be sure.

The Witch moved in with the family on the Bell farm in Robertson County in the early 1800s, and she lost no time in advertising her presence. Rarely has a ghost entered with such vitality into the life of a family and a community. She always joined the family in singing hymns, her shrill soprano piercing the air above the other voices, and at every revival meeting she shouted, shrieked, and moaned with a fervor unmatched for miles around.

The Witch would be the first to admit, however, that she was a pious fraud. It was suspected that her religious enthusiasm was inspired a good deal by corn whisky, which she consumed in great quantities when she wasn't stealing cream out of the Bells' icebox. She loved to show off her knowledge of the Bible, which she could recite verbatim. Nothing delighted the Witch more than to embarrass any preacher so rash as to argue Scripture with her, and it may be rightly assumed that she was more of a performer than a true believer.

The Witch took an instant dislike to John Bell, probably because she thought she was better qualified than he to direct the affairs of the family. She always spoke disparagingly of John to the other members of the family and took pleasure in cuffing him in the mouth from time to time. When John came down with a mysterious illness that made it difficult for him to swallow, the Witch was the prime suspect, and she made no attempt to defend herself.

On the other hand, the Witch adored Lucy, calling her "the most perfect woman on earth," and gave Mrs. Bell advice on household and financial matters. Since ghosts can travel much faster than jet planes, the Witch would often zoom off to North Carolina and come back with news and gossip about Lucy's relatives. The Witch could be very helpful when she wanted to be, and sometimes went to fetch the doctor or visit friends too far away for the Bells to contact, returning with information about their state of health. The Witch's enemies suspected, however, that she was less interested in giving service than in showing off her superhuman powers.

The Witch's concern for Lucy seemed to be genuine. When Mrs. Bell was ill, she would sob and moan, "Luce . . . poor Luce. . . ." The patient could not have had a more solicitous nurse. The Witch brought her strawberries, nuts, and grapes, cracking the nuts to make them easier for Lucy to eat. Once, when the rest of the family had gone off to a taffy pull during one of Lucy's illnesses, the Witch decided to punish them for deserting "poor Luce," and she literally "fixed their wagon." On the way, one of the wagon wheels mysteriously flew off, and John had no sooner put it back on than another wheel detached itself and rolled away. John got the message and took his disappointed children back to the farm.

The Witch seemed to have ambivalent feelings toward Betsy, sometimes criticizing her unmercifully, often showing her marked tenderness. Betsy, a beautiful girl, was courted by many young men, but the Witch disapproved of all of them. When the girl finally became engaged to handsome Joshua Gardner, the Witch pleaded with her not to marry him: "Betsy, please don't marry Joshua Gardner. Please don't marry him." When Betsy ignored her, the Witch became frantic and slapped the girl's cheeks. "I tell you, *don't* marry Joshua Gardner."

Poor Joshua himself was constantly hounded by the Witch, who vowed she would make life miserable for him if the marriage took place. Joshua was probably relieved when Betsy gave in and married her teacher, Richard Powell. The thought of being cursed and cuffed about for the rest of his life by the invisible Witch was probably too much for young Gardner, and even Betsy's good looks couldn't make up for it.

The Bell Witch's most famous confrontation was with another strong-minded character, Andrew Jackson. General Jackson had heard about the illustrious ghost and decided to investigate and do battle with her. He and his party came by wagon from Nashville for a week's stay at the Bell farm, but the Witch got in the first blow. Within sight of the Bell house, the wagon bogged down and the horses couldn't budge it. The impatient Jackson made his men get behind the wagon and shove, but they couldn't move it an inch. Suddenly a voice said, "All right, General, let the wagon move on. I will see you again tonight."

The Witch loved to stage-manage every situation. After Jackson and his men had unloaded their provisions and had a good dinner, they settled down in the parlor and waited for her to appear, but she was in no hurry. One of Jackson's men was the official "ghost-layer," and he waved his pistol in the light thrown by a solitary candle and bragged how he would shoot the ghost out of the house. After he had blustered for quite awhile, a voice said calmly, "All right, General, I am ready." Then the voice addressed the ghost-layer: "All right, Mr. Smarty. Here I am—shoot." The braggart jumped up and pulled the trigger in the direction of her voice, but the pistol wouldn't fire.

"Try again," taunted the Witch.

Again the pistol wouldn't fire. "Now," said the Bell Witch, "I'll teach you a lesson." The men heard the sound of an open hand whacking the ghost-layer, who went careening around the room, screaming, "She's got me by the nose." The door opened suddenly and the ghost-layer flew out of the house and away from the Bell farm.

Meanwhile Jackson rolled on the floor, convulsed with laughter, and roared, "Never had so much fun in all my life. This beats fighting the British." The Witch roared with him, then announced, "All right, General, I guess that's enough fun for tonight. You can go to bed now." Jackson, who was enjoying himself thoroughly, wanted to stay a full week, but his frightened men had had enough, and they insisted on leaving the next day.

John Bell died in 1820, and many people said the Witch hastened his death. The Witch herself left in 1828 and said she would come back in 107 years. So far she has not made good her promise, but there have been reports that she went to Mississippi and harangued another branch of the Bell family. There is a body of legend about her exploits with the Mississippi Bells, but those from Tennessee appear to be better authenticated. Members of the original Bell family and their descendants have written first- and secondhand accounts of the Witch.

Why did the Bell Witch leave in 1828 and why has she not returned? It may be that she doesn't have the same interest in the descendants of John Bell as she did in John, Lucy, and Betsy. In spite of her occasional mean tricks, the fun-loving ghost was fond of the Bells and considered herself one of the family.

GASPAR, THE
GALLANT GHOST

Gaspar first revealed himself to his host-family by appearing dramatically on a large rock near the water, wearing a flowing cloak and a broad-brimmed hat. He smiled, then disappeared.

The time was 1820, and the family had recently moved from England to a house in France on the outskirts of a seaport town. The family consisted of a mother and father, two young ladies, a boy of twelve, and an English servant. At first they thought Gaspar was a hallucination, but that night they heard someone scratching on the floor and repeated knocks on the wall.

They tried to ignore it. After all, all old houses made strange noises. But Gaspar was not to be ignored. At first he scratched under the window pane, then danced on the roof. Finally, the noises were concentrated in the bedroom where the two girls slept. They heard knocks on the wall, thirty to the minute, followed by a pause, then the thirty knocks were repeated.

The two girls, huddled in fear under the bedcovers, debated what to do. Was it a ghost, and if so, how could they find out? How does one know if a house is being haunted? The younger sister, eighteen years of age, suggested that they ask the ghost point-blank whether he was a ghost. Enough of this scary business.

"If you are indeed a ghost," the intrepid young lady said in a loud, clear voice, "knock six times."

Gaspar obliged with six knocks.

The matter being settled, the girls went to sleep. The next evening everybody gathered in the drawing room to sing French songs, with the elder sister playing the piano accompaniment. The voices of the three women and the little boy were in the soprano range, but now they were joined by a low, resonant voice that took the bass part. When the song was over, this voice spoke.

"Welcome, messieurs and mesdames, to your new home. My name is Gaspar, and I hope you will allow me to visit you from time to time."

Although Gaspar was invisible, they all thought he was charming and invited him to come as often as he liked. Gaspar entered with Gallic enthusiasm into the activities of the family. Not only did he sing with great feeling, but he recited poetry in a deep, dramatic voice. He was also something of a moralist and often, when the family was seated around the fire in the living room, he would regale his captive audience with lectures on virtue and harmony.

Soon he was calling each member of the family by his or her first name. And, like the Bell Witch but far more gracious than the persecutor of John Bell, he was free with advice on domestic and social matters. Gaspar seemed to know the answer to any question. Whenever there was a dispute, the ghost settled it. He would dogmatically announce, "M—— is wrong; S—— is right."

Gaspar was unfailingly polite, yet, being invisible, would often startle the family when he spoke. Finally, the young son said, "Gaspar, I should like to see you." Gaspar materialized, smiling and wearing the same large cloak and broad-brimmed hat he had first appeared in. Then he vanished, as before.

When the family had been in France for three years, Gaspar announced that he was about to leave on a three-month trip, but not to despair—he would return. When asked where he was going, he was silent, as he was whenever the family pressed him for information about himself. Three months later Gaspar returned and said in his theatrical voice: "I am with you again."

The time finally came for the family to return to England, and Gaspar, like the ghost in Count Hamon's house, decided he wanted to go along. After a brief stay in Suffolk, however, he told them regretfully that it would not work out—he must go back to France. He explained that their community was not yet ready to accept a ghost who had the run of the house, and that the French were more tolerant of this kind of situation. If he remained, Gaspar pointed out, the family would surely suffer. There were tearful goodbyes as Gaspar took his leave.

The story of Gaspar was told to a gentleman by the younger of the two sisters and eventually appeared in Robert Dale Owen's *Footfalls on the Boundary of Another World*. Who was Gaspar? He would tell nothing about himself. His only motive was that he enjoyed sharing the family life of his English friends.

PARTY-LOVING
GHOSTS

Everhope is a red brick house in Mississippi, built in 1841 by Andrew Knox. Knox had a son of whom he was proud, and he was determined that when the boy grew up and married, there would be a gala celebration that the state of Mississippi would never forget. While the house was being built, Knox had bottles of wine sealed in the walls, to be opened on his son's wedding day.

Unfortunately, the boy died before reaching adulthood, and Knox sold the house. But on a December night some years later, a group of party-loving ghosts arrived at the house all set for a spirit-wedding. When they had assembled, the walls slowly opened and the bottles of wine danced out and jumped on silver platters. As the ghost guests downed their drinks, the glasses kept filling up with the precious red liquid—up to the very top. At midnight the ghosts departed and the bottles, still full of wine, hopped back to their perches inside the walls. The walls closed up and there was silence—until the following December, when another celebration took place.

Many ghosts are fond of liquor. Robert Graves, the writer, involuntarily shared a glass of whisky with a ghost who showed up in North Wales one New Year's Eve. Other ghosts have assisted at parties, serving highballs and cocktails. The ghosts at the 18th-century New Year's Eve party, described in the chapter on friendly musical ghosts, had plenty of wine to drink. The Bell Witch, who had about as much fun as any ghost, always drank her corn whisky with great gusto. Where does the liquor go when the ghost has imbibed it? No one really knows, but neither does anyone know where ghosts come from and disappear to.

[VI]

GHOSTLY GUARDIANS
AND ADVISORS

The history of ghosts indicates that each of us is accompanied at all times by a spirit who sees that we don't get into trouble or make the wrong decisions. This ghost stays discreetly in the background and makes no attempt to interfere with our daily activities until there is a crisis. Then he appears dramatically and tells us to change direction quickly at peril of death, injury, or other bad fortune. Most of us don't take our guardian ghosts seriously, however, and as a result we constantly find ourselves in difficulties. The classic example, described in this chapter, is that of James IV of Scotland, who went to a certain death that could have been avoided if he had listened to his ghost.

Guardian ghosts have stepped up their activities in the modern era, trying to prevent accidents in autos, planes, trains, and ships. Countess Lillimay Kobylanska, writing in Eileen Garrett's *Beyond The Five Senses,* tells about being awakened early one morning and instructed to cancel her reservation on the 1 o'clock train. She took another train and heard later that the 1 o'clock train had been wrecked. In another instance a guardian ghost directed a man to take the 10 o'clock train and no other. In Australia, a gentleman was visited twice by his guardian ghost, once on land and again at sea, and warned not to transfer to another ship. The warning probably saved his life, because most of the passengers on the second ship died of food poisoning.

The air above the oceans must be filled with guardian ghosts who hover benevolently over ships and appear with warnings if disaster is imminent. Often they are the spirits of captains who had commanded a particular ship during life and continue to guide it after they have died. According to a Chinese legend, the dead captain of a war junk who had been murdered by pirates appeared to the new commander of the ship and told him how to elude the pirates. As in so many instances of ghosts at sea, he was accompanied by mystical lights.

In ancient times, guardian ghosts were known as daemons, and their presence was accepted without question by the most thoughtful of men. Socrates, who required a great deal of convincing in other matters, always turned a willing ear to the advice offered by his friendly daemon. Daniel Defoe tells how the daemon of Julius Caesar "gave hints to him that he was in danger" but Caesar, like James IV and so many other historical figures, ignored the warning and, in Defoe's words, "neglecting his own Safety . . . he goes into the Senate, and is murder'd." We are indebted to the Roman writer Dio Cassius for the story of the emperor Trajan, who was trapped in a building in Antioch during an earthquake in 99 A.D. Trajan's guardian ghost led him out of a window to safety.

What is more natural than that the ghostly guardian of children should be the spirit of their mother, if she is not living? There are many stories, including the one in this chapter, about such spirits who appear just in time to prevent an accident to their children. There are also guardian ghosts who stay in a particular locale where disasters occur and give advance notice of trouble to all who come into the area. The famous Gray Man of the Carolinas is one of these.

SOCRATES AND HIS WISE SPIRIT

If the Greek philosopher Socrates was a calm man, always sure of himself and his ideas, it may be that the presence of his daemon was responsible. According to Plato, Socrates said that he was "moved by a certain divine and spiritual influence. . . . This began with me from childhood, being a kind of voice, which, when present, always diverts me from what I am about to do. . . ."

Socrates' ghostly advisor extended his protective interest to the philosopher's friends and acquaintances and always knew in advance if there was any trouble in store for them. On one occasion Socrates was attending a dinner with his friend Timarchus. As the latter rose to leave, the ghost whispered a warning in Socrates' ear. Socrates turned to Timarchus and told him to sit down, that there was danger waiting outside. Timarchus sat down but rose again a bit later, and the warning was repeated. But he was anxious to leave, and he finally sneaked off—only to commit a murder for which he was later executed. Before dying, Timarchus admitted that he should have heeded the words of the guardian ghost.

Plutarch gives an example of how the daemon protected Socrates and his friends from trivial annoyances as well as from danger. Once the philosopher was strolling through Athens with a group of friends when the guardian ghost whispered in his ear that he should go down another street. Socrates turned down a side street, accompanied by part of the group, but the rest laughed at his warning and continued on their way. The scoffers were later set upon by stampeding pigs, who knocked them down and bruised both their persons and their egos.

Except for his wife Xanthippe, whose sharp tongue generally drove him out of the house, no one could get the best of Socrates in a debate, a fact that annoyed the politicians and lesser philosophers of Athens. It was finally decided that the daemon was turning Socrates into a dangerous radical, and he was brought to trial. The guardian ghost had warned him this would happen and predicted he would end up as a martyr. When Socrates was about to prepare a speech in his defense, the ghost advised him to submit without protest. He took his sentencing calmly and told the judges: "I think that what has happened to me has been a good thing; and we must have been mistaken when we supposed that death was an evil."

Socrates used his skill as a debater to prove the immortality of the soul, and he may have been encouraged in this belief by his daemon. The premonitions of his guardian ghost convinced him that the future could be divined, and he gave serious attention to the predictions of the Greek oracles. We know that he often advised his disciples to consult the Delphic oracle.

Socrates may have been partial to the oracles because they flattered him. According to Plato, his friend Cherephon once asked the Pythia if there was anyone in the world wiser than Socrates. The oracle replied that no such man existed.

THE KING WHO
WOULDN'T LISTEN

If ever a guardian ghost had his hands full, it was the kindly spirit who watched over James IV of Scotland. James was rather more foolish than the average king and was always getting into trouble. He had so many weaknesses that his ghost had trouble keeping track of them, and possibly the worst was that his head could be turned by flattery, especially the blandishments of his nobles and the clergy. When they assured him that a military expedition against England would result in a glorious victory, James put the country on a war footing and prepared to march.

The guardian ghost knew otherwise, but James didn't pay any attention to him. According to Defoe in his *History and Reality of Apparitions*, the desperate ghost finally donned a bizarre disguise, hoping this would work with the impressionable king. On the evening before the army was to march, James attended services in the Royal Chapel of his Palace. While he was praying—for military victory, no doubt—there appeared before him "an ancient Man . . .

with a long Head of Hair of the Colour of Amber . . . and of a venerable Aspect, having on a rustick Dress . . . a belted Plaid girdled round with a Linen Sash."

The disguised ghost told James that, if he knew what was good for him, he'd better not do battle with the British. Nor was that all, the ghost continued, looking over his list of James' sins. He warned the lascivious king to "abstain from his Lewd and Unchristian Practices with wicked Women, for that if he did not, it would issue in his Destruction. . . ."

Since James IV liked nothing better than to fight wars and keep company with strumpets, he ignored the advice. The next morning he marched with his army until he reached Jedburgh, where he fell to "drinking Wine very plentifully in a great Hall of the House. . . ." The ghost materialized again and told the king in unmistakable terms that "he was sent . . . to warn him, not to proceed in that War." Not only would James lose the battle, said the ghost, but also his crown and his kingdom.

This second appearance gave James pause, but by now the wine had gone to his head, the women were more pleasing than ever, and the prospect of soundly thrashing the British army was too tempting to forego. He ordered his army to continue its march. Perhaps he thought the ghost was some kind of English trick, but if so, he should have had more respect for the British and their resourcefulness.

The inevitable happened, as it always does when friendly warnings from ghosts are ignored. James not only lost the war; he perished at Flodden Field. Defoe ends his account with this acid comment: "I need say no more of it."

THE GOOD GHOST
OF THE CAROLINAS

Pawley's Island is an old resort area off the mainland of South Carolina. It is a haven for those on a holiday, very pleasant in calm weather, with its long expanse of sandy beach and its scrub oaks, cedars, and myrtles. But the weather can be treacherous, and violent storms often arise with little or no warning. Moreover, the Island is directly in the path of hurricanes that roar up along the coast from the Caribbean.

The Gray Man is the guardian ghost of Pawley's Island. He knows when a storm is approaching, and if he thinks it may endanger the lives of visitors from the mainland or those living on the Island, he appears to them, often in symbolic form, and they pack up and leave until the danger is past.

The Island has been devastated by three classic storms—one in 1822, another in 1893, and Hurricane Hazel in 1954. The Gray Man materialized before each one. One day in 1893 there was a knock on the door of a French family called the Lachicottes, and a strange-looking creature enveloped in a kind of gray mist stood there. He asked them for bread, and they knew at once that this was a warning of danger and left immediately for the mainland. The storm that followed is still spoken of as one of the worst in South Carolina history.

The Gray Man has been watching over Pawley's Island for almost 150 years. He appears mostly in late September or October, when he is seen strolling along the beach. In April, 1954, a family of tourists saw a medium-sized man dressed in gray walking slowly along the water's edge. Then he vanished. The next day Hurricane Hazel swept over the Island.

It is also said that no harm will come to those who see him, or to their homes, even if they stay on the Island during the storm. The day before Hurricane Hazel arrived, a homeowner on the Island was fast asleep when at 5 A.M. he heard a loud pounding on the door. A stranger was standing there—an old man dressed in gray clothes whom the homeowner had never seen before. The stranger said that the Red Cross had sent him around to warn everyone to leave the Island. Then he disappeared. Although most of the houses on the Island were destroyed in the hurricane, this man's home was not touched.

Who the Gray Man is, or who he was when alive, is open to conjecture. There are legends about him dating back two hundred years, and in every one he is the tragic hero of a love story that ended unhappily. In the early 1800s a South Carolina beauty became engaged to a young man who subsequently sank to his death in one of the treacherous marshes between the Island and the mainland. In 1822, when the young lady was walking along the beach, he appeared in a gray mist. The storm broke two days later.

Perhaps the earliest version of the Gray Man placed him in the pre-Revolutionary era, when a young girl in Charleston fell in love with her unworthy cousin. To break up the romance, the family sent the young man to Europe, and a report came back later that he had been killed. The broken-hearted girl married a wealthy man, and they built a summer home on Pawley's Island called the "Island Home."

One day in 1778 the young man, very much alive, walked into the Island Home, and the young lady fainted. Shortly thereafter, he went by sea from Pawley's Island to Charleston, contracted yellow fever, and died. In the years that followed he was seen many times near the Island Home, lurking in the undergrowth around the house. He is still seen there today and is thought by many to be the same Gray Man who appears on the beach just before a storm.

The earliest stories about the Gray Man were told by owners of plantations in the Carolinas and by their slaves and the fishermen who came to Pawley's Island to ply their trade. Stories are still coming in from present-day visitors and residents. Until gale winds and torrential rains cease to put the Island in jeopardy, the Gray Man will be there, walking up and down the beach for all to see and take heed.

THE SPIRIT
WHO SAVED
THE CHILDREN

The story of the children and the open well was first told in a 19th-century book called *Ghostly Visitors*. The wife of a well-to-do gentleman died, and the latter was left with the care of four young children. Because the house they lived in held so many sad memories, the father sold it and purchased a home out in the country. This was a very old and large, rambling mansion with so many floors and rooms that it took weeks to properly explore it.

When the family moved in, they found that only one section of the house was livable, and even the rooms in this section would have to be put in order. For several weeks, the father was busy having the rooms cleaned out and redecorated. He bought new furniture, had the floors thoroughly scrubbed and the walls repapered, and called in carpenters and plumbers to make repairs. The subterranean rooms and passages in the mansion would have to wait many months before he could look at them.

The children, however, enjoyed exploring the mysterious gloomy rooms and dark corridors that had probably been untouched for a hundred years or more. They ran up and down rickety stairs, pulled open creaky doors that had been closed for decades, and peeked into musty closets and cellars. One afternoon they ventured into an old room thick with dust and grime and, to their delight, found in it a spiral staircase that came up from below through the middle of the room and ascended to another level. Squealing and giggling, the children ran up the stairway into the room above.

This room was very large and very depressing. The sun was completely cut off by sealed windows almost black with layers of dirt. An old, moth-eaten rug covered the expanse of floor, while faded tapestries hung from the wall. Large portraits of stern-looking ladies and gentlemen from another era stared down disapprovingly at the children. What frightened them most, however, were huge pictures of mythological animals—dragons with forked tongues, enormous sea serpents, and monsters with curved talons that seemed to reach out at the children.

Panic-stricken, the children screamed and hurried down the staircase, led by the eldest, an eight-year-old girl. But in their anxiety to get away, they ran past the room below and descended into pitch blackness.

Suddenly, the eight-year-old stopped and stepped back in fear, crying, "Mama!" A shadowy figure loomed in the darkness ahead of her. It was her dead mother, frantically signalling her to go back up the stairs.

"It is Mama! I see Mama and she waves us back."

The children, now in a state of terror, ran back up the stairs and found their father on the main floor; they excitedly told him that they had seen their mother. The father lit a candle and went down the staircase, past the room on the upper level and into the darkness below. At the foot of the stairs, a few feet from where his oldest girl had stood, he saw an open well.

In their hasty descent, the children would have pitched into the well and probably been killed—had not the guardian ghost of their mother appeared to warn them.

GHOSTS ON EMERGENCY CALL

Spirits are as concerned as the rest of us about persons who are ill, and they do all they can to help out. Many doctors return as ghosts to give instructions to their colleagues or to those who are nursing the sick. Sometimes the spirit doctor will speak or act directly through the voice and body of a live person, as in many cases of psychic surgery. Edgar Cayce, who in a state of trance made diagnoses and prescribed remedies for ailing persons often hundreds of miles away, may have been helped by medical authorities in the invisible world. Cayce, a layman who knew nothing about medicine when awake, showed an astonishing knowledge of anatomy while in a trance.

Some ghosts, who were not doctors or nurses when in their bodies, seem to acquire medical knowledge in the spirit world. One of these was the lady ghost who prescribed coffee and limes for her bedridden sister, a case discussed in this chapter. Other ghosts go off to summon doctors or priests on behalf of a desperately ill person or one who is dying and needs spiritual comfort. Sometimes they appear directly to the doctor or priest, and at other times they call on the telephone.

Elliott O'Donnell tells the story of a doctor who answered his telephone and was told by a voice he did not recognize that a friend of his was very ill and needed him at once. When he arrived at his friend's home, the servant was surprised to see him and said that his master was in good health. Both the servant and the friend thought it was a social call. Moments later, however, the friend suffered a burst blood vessel, and the doctor, acting quickly, was able to save his life. No one in the house had called the doctor, nor had there been any reason to do so, since the friend was in perfect health when he arrived.

There are two very strange cases about ghosts on emergency call which do not fit into any of the above categories. In one, a man's own ghost detached itself from his body and went in search of help when he was in danger of dying. The story, investigated by the Society for Psychical Research, is about an Englishman of the last century, Mr. Varley, who put himself to sleep each night with a sponge saturated with chloroform, which he held to his nose as he lay in bed. One night, as he was doing this, he became unconscious and was in danger of being asphyxiated. His ghost, aware of what was happening, went into another room where his wife was sleeping and woke her up, and she came running into the room and removed the sponge.

The other case, reported in the *New York Post* of May 6, 1969, comes from the city of Karachi, in Pakistan. A 2½-year-old girl apparently died, and she was buried. As her mother slept that night, a spirit came to her and said, "Go and dig the grave and you will find your child alive." The mother, accompanied by a curious crowd, went to the grave the next day, opened it, and found the child sitting in her coffin and smiling brightly.

A GHOST VISITS
THE DOCTOR

It had been an exhausting day, and the doctor wanted to retire and get some much-needed rest. He had been to the hospital in the morning, attending to a few serious postoperative cases, and there were several home calls in the afternoon and early evening. The doctor turned up the heat, for it was a very cold night, took a shower, got a book from the library, and crawled into bed. After reading for about half an hour, he dozed off.

He was awakened by the insistent ringing of the front doorbell, but he was too tired to get up. Whatever business his caller had in mind would have to wait until morning. He turned over and began to doze again. But as he slept, the bell kept ringing and continued to buzz intermittently for fifteen minutes.

Shivering, the doctor got out of bed, put on his bathrobe and slippers, and stumbled toward the front door. He looked at his watch and saw that it was 1 A.M. A poor time to wake someone up, even if he was a physician.

"Yes, yes," he called impatiently as the doorbell kept ringing. He opened the door, admitting a blast of cold air, and saw to his great surprise a small girl about nine years old, very thin and pale, dressed in old, nondescript clothes, with a frayed shawl around her shoulders.

"Please, doctor," said the girl. "My mother is very ill. Will you go to her?"

How the child had found her way through the blinding snow and bitter cold, the doctor couldn't guess. He felt sorry for her, but he was very tired.

"Try some other doctor," he said. "I have a very full day tomorrow, and I must get my rest."

"But I don't know any other doctor," said the girl. "My mother wants only you."

The doctor said no once again, but he knew he would eventually give in. There was something so touchingly pathetic about this thin little girl and her concern for her mother that, weary as he was, he could not refuse her.

"Well, come in, come in," he said brusquely. She hesitated, and he took her arm and led her to a large, overstuffed chair. "Now you sit there and warm up, otherwise you'll be ill, too. I'll get dressed."

The doctor put on his heavy overcoat, got his black bag, and took the girl in his car to a tenement district, where she led him to a very old, decayed building with a narrow hallway that was barely lit. They climbed several flights of stairs.

The girl's mother was lying in bed in a small, dark room. Her eyes lit up when the doctor walked in, and he recognized her as a former servant of his. She was very weak, and her temperature was at the danger point. The doctor telephoned an all-night pharmacist and told him to send over without delay a medicine that would bring down her fever.

Seeing the mother so ill, the doctor was glad he had come. He looked around for the little girl, but she was not in the room.

"You have a very intelligent and considerate daughter," he told his patient. "It took courage to go out on a night like this and find a doctor."

The woman frowned.

"But I have no children. My only daughter died a month ago. Her clothes are over there in the closet."

The doctor recalled that the child had not entered the room with him, and he had not seen her all the time he was attending her mother. He opened the closet door and saw hanging there the same threadbare coat and shawl he had noticed on the girl, and on the floor the shoes she had been wearing. The clothes and shoes were warm and dry and obviously had not been used for some time.

The doctor was S. Weir Mitchell, a Philadelphia neurologist. The story has been told many times, first by Dr. Mitchell and then by others who marveled at the miracle of the little girl ghost who responded to her mother's emergency call.

GHOST GUIDES
IN A STORM

This story about a pair of ghost dogs on emergency call was told to me by writer Ralph L. Woods, and it happened to his grandfather.

Dr. John J. O'Brien was the last person Ralph or anyone else would have expected to be involved with ghosts. He was a huge man with a red beard and a hearty laugh— a man as down-to-earth as a country doctor could and should be. Perhaps it was the Irish strain in him that appealed to the ghosts. Dr. O'Brien was born and grew up in Ireland, and it may be that he had made the acquaintance of gremlins and spirits as a child, although he never said so.

The O'Briens were adventurous souls. After graduating from medical school in Dublin, John thought it would be fun to see the world, then settle down and practice medicine in Australia. While travelling through America, he met a young lady named Elizabeth Fitzwilliam and asked her to marry him. Then it occurred to him that there were just as many sick people in America as in Australia, and he decided to stay in the St. Louis area and heal patients there.

He bought a home on a hill for Elizabeth near the city, made a down payment on a horse and buggy, and devoted the rest of his life to the ailing folk whose little cabins and cottages were spread over the countryside for miles around. Dr. O'Brien was the typical country doctor at the turn of the century, and his heart was as big as his body. He had a warm bedside manner and the kind of cheerful Irish wit that did his patients as much good as the medicines in his black bag. And he could be very forgetful about sending bills to those who were struggling for a living.

If Dr. O'Brien was psychic, it may be because he had empathy with his patients in a day when the human relationship between doctor and patient made up for a lack of antibiotics and other wonder drugs. He kept getting "feelings" about his patients and their condition. It was a time before telephones were in general use, and doctors had to rely on their sixth sense to tell them when their patients needed them.

One night in mid-winter during a violent storm (somehow people in those days always needed their doctors when the weather was particularly bad), Dr. O'Brien remarked to his wife over dinner that he had not seen Mrs. Kilpatrick for quite awhile. Mrs. Kilpatrick was an elderly lady with a weak heart who spent most of her days in bed. Tonight Dr. O'Brien had a feeling that he should see her.

It was a mean night to take the horse out, but the doctor would never forgive himself if his patient needed him and he did not come.

He tried to put the feeling aside, but it would not go away. The house was nice and warm, with logs crackling cheerily in the fireplace, but outside he could hear the wind whistling while snow pelted the windows and blanketed the yard. Reluctantly, he put on his heavy overcoat and fur-lined gloves, pulled on his overshoes, covered his neck and face with the warm woolen scarf Elizabeth had made for him, took his little black bag, and went to the stable to get the horse. He patted the nag's face, then hitched her to the buggy.

It was a ride Dr. O'Brien would never forget. Mrs. Kilpatrick's house was several miles away, and it took a lot of twisting and turning down side roads to find it. It had always been daylight and good weather when he went there before, but now, as icy winds blew snow into his face, and drifts piled up in front and at the side of the road, Dr. O'Brien lost his way. So thick was the blizzard, he could not see three feet in front of the buggy and not at all to the right or left. Where should he make the first turn? It was impossible to know when he passed another road.

Then he heard the faint sound of a dog barking, a sound that grew louder. No, there was more than one dog. Now, just ahead of him, he saw through the swirling snow two giant mastiffs, one on either side of the buggy and just in front of the horse. They were leading the way and barking. The doctor sensed that they wanted him to follow them. Suddenly they turned to the left, and the doctor turned with them. Sure enough, it was a road, and the dogs continued down it, barking as they ran. Another half mile and they turned to the right, the horse and buggy following.

Did these dogs belong to Mrs. Kilpatrick, and had they come to guide him to the house? He didn't recall that she had a dog, nor could he think of anyone else in the area who had two mastiffs. Still, he had no choice but to follow them. What other reason could they have for being out on a night like this except to guide him and his horse? Providence, reflected the doctor, does move in mysterious ways.

More twists and turns, down one road a little way, then another road to the right, one to the left, another one to the left, then a short jog to the right, and there it was—Mrs. Kilpatrick's little wooden house, now completely covered with snow and ice. Through the snow-caked window he could see a light burning. He got out his black bag and trudged to the door. He banged the knocker.

Mr. Kilpatrick opened the door and invited him in.

"I'm so glad to see you, doctor. The missus has been doing badly all day, and she has trouble breathing. But here, let's get your clothes dry, and warm your hands by the fire."

He took the doctor's overcoat and boots. Dr. O'Brien slapped his hands in front of the fire a few times, then went into the bedroom to see his patient. Her pulse was very low and her breathing was labored. He gave her some medicine for her heart, then something to put her to sleep. Soon she was breathing more easily, and she dropped off into a restful slumber.

Mr. Kilpatrick wouldn't let the doctor go out into the storm just yet. First his clothes would have to dry and he should have some hot coffee and food. Dr. O'Brien, weary from the strain of finding his way in the storm, was glad to relax for awhile in the rocking-chair.

Suddenly he remembered the mastiffs. He had not heard them barking.

"Where are your dogs, Mr. Kilpatrick?"

The old man was puzzled. He had no dogs. No, none of the neighbors had mastiffs.

About 4 A.M. the storm was over. The roads were covered with deep drifts, but at least the moon was out and Dr. O'Brien would be able to find his way home. He rode home slowly but saw no dogs and heard no barking.

For several days thereafter, Dr. O'Brien inquired

around the countryside about the mastiffs. No one had such dogs or knew of anyone else who did. It was certainly a mystery, but there was one remaining thought that kept bothering Dr. O'Brien.

When he had stopped his horse and buggy in front of the Kilpatricks' house, the dogs had seemed to vanish— just melted away. At the time, he had thought it was because he had trouble seeing in the blizzard. Now he had another explanation. The two mastiffs had been sent or had come as spirit guides in the storm—ghost dogs on emergency call.

THE MYSTERIOUS
PHONE CALL

Many ghostologists have told stories about doctors and priests who received telephone calls in the middle of the night and hastened to patients who needed them, only to find out that no living person had put a call through. The ghost in this story did not communicate by phone himself but presumably took a message which he delivered to a priest. The case was described in the *Westminster Cathedral Chronicle* of March, 1919, and later investigated by the Society for Psychical Research.

It had been Father Brompton's intention, when he first went to his dying parishioner's home, to give her the Last Sacrament. She was suffering from an incurable disease, and now it was just a matter of time until the end, perhaps just hours. But when he arrived early in the evening, he was met at the door by the doctor, who asked him not to see the patient just yet. Would he please wait until morning? Father Brompton agreed, but he was not easy in his mind about the delay. He left the telephone number of the Oratory with the nurse and told her to call him immediately if the patient wanted him.

Father Brompton went back to the Oratory and got into bed, thinking about the dying lady. As a devout Catholic, it would be a serious matter for her to expire without having a priest in attendance. Father Brompton tossed restlessly on his bed, and prayed that she would be spared until he could visit her in the morning and give her last rites. Then he dropped off into a deep sleep.

A few hours later the priest heard the door of the room open softly. He looked up and saw a dark-robed figure standing by the door, and he thought it was the father in charge at the Oratory.

"Is that you, Father?" he asked sleepily.

The figure muttered something about a telephone call, but Father Brompton could not hear him and asked him to speak louder.

"Be quick!" said the dark-robed man in a clearer voice. "There is no time to lose. There has been a phone call—go to the dying patient."

With that, the man seemed to vanish. Father Brompton rubbed his eyes sleepily, then got out of bed, noting by his watch that it was a quarter to four. He dressed hastily, then went downstairs. Outside he walked briskly until he came to his destination. He rang the bell several times, but there was no answer, although the lights were on in the house. After much ringing and banging on the door, it was finally opened by the nurse.

"Oh, doctor, it's good that you are here," she said. "The patient is much worse."

Father Brompton reminded the nurse that he was the priest, not the doctor. As he walked through the living room, he heard the patient say from her bed, "If only Father Brompton would come." The nurse said she had been asking for him for about half an hour. He administered last rites, and the patient died an hour later.

As he was leaving the house, he said to the nurse, "I'm so glad you called me. Otherwise I would have been too late."

"But I didn't call you," replied the puzzled nurse. "I called the doctor."

In the morning Father Brompton asked the father in

charge if he had come to the bedroom the night before with a telephone message.

"No, Father, I never left my room last night. There was no telephone call."

Father Brompton then contacted the telephone exchange for the Oratory. The records were checked, but no call had been put through to the Oratory the night before. Nor had the doctor on the case attempted to reach him.

Father Brompton concluded that a spirit on emergency call had roused him. The ghost, knowing that even telephone messages can go astray, had decided to take the appeal of the dying patient directly to the priest.

AN INVISIBLE NURSE

Mr. Paige knew that his wife would die in a few months. He knew it because the doctors had said so and because she was suffering from cancer, for which there was no cure. He knew it also because Maria, his wife's sister, had told him. Maria was no longer living, but she was still concerned about her sister and had taken on the role of spirit nurse to make Eliza Anne's last days more comfortable.

When Maria first appeared through a medium, she told Mr. Paige: "Within three days Eliza Anne will say she has seen me and Mother." Mr. Paige said nothing to his wife or anyone else, but three days later the live nurse came running in and said that Eliza Anne was delirious, that she had sprung out of bed calling Maria by name and had run toward the door, crying, "Stop, Maria! Stop, Mother! Don't go yet!"

As Eliza Anne grew worse, her pain increased. She could keep no food on her stomach and was in great distress and unable to sleep. Maria told Mr. Paige to brew some very strong coffee at a high temperature, add plenty of cream and sugar, and give it to the patient with some cream toast. Eliza Anne ate the toast and drank the coffee with much relish, then fell into a deep, restful sleep.

She stayed with this diet for several days and was in less pain and able to sleep soundly. Gradually, however, the pain began to come back, and once again no food would stay in her stomach. Maria was consulted again and she gave a new prescription: "Give Eliza Anne pure juice of lime every day. This will give her an appetite and she will be able to retain the food she eats."

For a long period of time Eliza Anne was free of pain, and she enjoyed her daily lime juice and the nourishing food that followed it. But as Maria and the doctors had said, it was only a matter of time. Gradually she began to fade again, and Mr. Paige knew that the end was not far off. Maria told him: "The next time she says she has seen me, do not leave her."

A few days later Mr. Paige went into the sickroom at 2 A.M. to relieve the nurse, who told him that Eliza Anne had seen Maria again. While he watched at her bedside, she suddenly said, "I must go." Then she died.

The case of Eliza Anne Paige and Maria was described in the Proceedings of the Society for Psychical Research. One of the Society's investigators, Richard Hodgson, interviewed Mr. Paige and was satisfied that he was a sincere man who believed he had been in contact with Maria. Besides, whatever Maria had said proved to be right, and her prescriptions as a ghost nurse had helped Eliza Anne through the difficult period when her body was dying.

[VIII]

GHOSTS IN SEARCH OF JUSTICE

If a ghost has been appearing to you from time to time and behaving oddly, be patient. Wait and see what he wants to tell you. He may be one of those spirits with a strong sense of justice who has chosen you to correct some wrong that was done to him while in the flesh. In most instances he will choose a relative or friend for the assignment, but sometimes ghosts will tap a stranger on the shoulder and ask him to be their intermediary. During the Puritan era, many a farmer working in his fields was interrupted by a ghost and told to put aside his plow and go looking for a murderer.

There have also been cases of apparent suicides who came back as ghosts to set the record straight and clear their good names. The ghost of Robert Mackenzie visited his employer in a dream and told him there would be a report that the young man had committed suicide but that the report was false. Subsequent investigation proved that Mackenzie had mistakenly drunk a bottle of nitric acid. Another and more famous case was that of a naval officer who was beaten to death by two fellow officers. The Navy had listed him as a suicide, but his ghost came to his mother and warned her not to believe the official version. Professor James H. Hyslop, who taught logic, made an exhaustive study of the case and concluded that the Navy version was false. Marks on the boy's exhumed body proved that the account given to his mother was correct.

Ghosts are concerned that money and property they have left behind go to their rightful heirs, but this does not always happen. Thomas Harris wrote what he thought was a perfectly valid will (discussed later in this chapter), but the combination of a greedy brother and a legal technicality threatened to leave his four children penniless. Harris took the unusual step of composing a new will in the spirit world that verified what his intention had been before dying, then seeking out a reliable friend to deliver the substance of it to the court.

TWO PURITAN GHOSTS

To a hard-working Puritan, going about his business of raising crops and storing jam for the winter, it must have been disconcerting to have a ghost appear and ask him to drop everything and become involved in a murder case. The *New England Weekly Journal* of December 1, 1729, published this news item:

"Last week, one belonging to Ipswich came to Boston and related that some time since he was at Canso in Nova Scotia, and that on a certain day there appeared to him an apparition in blood and wounds, and told him that at such a time and place, mentioning both, he was barbarously murdered by one, who was at Rhode Island, and desired him to go to the said person and charge him with the said murder, and prosecute him therefor, naming several circumstances relating to the murder; and that since his arrival from Canso to Ipswich the said apparition had appeared to him again, and urged him immediately to prosecute the said affair. The abovesaid person having related the matter was advised and encouraged to go to Rhode Island and engage therein, and he accordingly set out for that place on Thursday last."

There is no further word about what happened when the ghost's deputy confronted the alleged killer in Rhode Island. What would a peace-loving Puritan do in a situation like this? "One belonging to Ipswich" must have been quite nervous, not being sure how the accused man might react. He had, however, the choice of bringing the murderer to justice or risking repeated visitations from the ghost in "blood and wounds."

Stern old Cotton Mather, a Puritan clergyman and writer, pondered at some length over what should be done about ghosts who suddenly materialized and pointed an accusing finger at some innocent-appearing member of the community. Finally, he made this ruling: "When there has been a murder committed, an apparition of the slain party accusing of any man, although such apparitions have oftener spoke true than false, is not enough to convict the man of that murder; but yet it is a sufficient occasion for Magistrates to make a particular inquiry."

In one case that came to Cotton Mather's attention, the ghost of a murdered man travelled 3,000 miles from London to Boston to inform his brother that he had been foully slain and to request that justice be done. Mather writes in his *Wonders of the Invisible World* that on May 2, 1687, a Mr. Joseph Beacon woke up at 5 A.M. and saw his brother standing at his bedside with a napkin "tyed about his Head" and a "bloody Wound on one side of his Forehead."

The two brothers exchanged greetings and then Joseph, wondering what had brought his brother all the way from London, asked, "What's the Matter, Brother? How came you here?"

His brother's ghost replied: "Brother, I have been most barbarously and injuriously Butchered, by a Debauched Drunken Fellow, to whom I never did any wrong in my Life. . . ." He warned that the murderer was planning to change his name and escape to New England. "I would pray you . . . to get an Order from the Governor, to Seize the Person, whom I have now described; and then do you Indict him for the Murder of me, your Brother." The murdered man reassured Joseph that he would personally "prove the Indictment," although he didn't explain what kind of persuasion he would use on the judge. Then the ghost faded away.

At the end of June news came from London verifying that the brother had been killed. He had had a date with a young lady and had gone to call a coach, when he was accosted by "a Fellow with a Fire-fork," who wounded him in the skull. He died on May 2 at 5 A.M.

The end of the story, unfortunately, offers no comfort to those on the side of justice. The murderer was caught before he could sneak off to America, but, as was the custom in those days, he bribed his captors to let him go. Today, he couldn't buy his way out. On the other hand, a modern court would not admit the testimony of the murdered man even though, in the words of the ghost, he would stand by and "prove the Indictment."

A GHOST ON THE WITNESS STAND

The perfect witness at a murder trial, of course, would be the murdered man himself. Ghosts know, however, that they just can't stroll into a courtroom and ask to testify in their own behalf. For one thing, the ghost might not be seen by all of those present, and those who did see him would be detained by the judge for observation. And even if it was perfectly obvious to everyone that a ghost was there, the court psychiatrist would prove with expert testimony that it was a collective hallucination.

Ghosts in search of justice, therefore, usually have the good sense to tell their story to a third party whose integrity would be respected in court. Often there is corroborating evidence that backs up the ghost's charges. There is one case, however, described by Daniel Defoe in *History and Reality of Apparitions,* of a ghost who did appear in court as a prosecution witness and helped to convict his own murderer.

A murder had been committed and a suspect brought to trial. The accused man pleaded not guilty, and as there were no witnesses and no circumstantial evidence, the judge, although he was sure the man was guilty, feared he might have to release him. The man was shifty-eyed and nervous but had been cunning enough to leave no clues.

While the prisoner was standing at the bar, earnestly protesting his innocence, he gave a sudden start and turned pale, a fact that did not go unnoticed by the astute judge. He stared at the witness stand for a moment, then shook a quivering finger at it and said, "That is not fair, 'tis not according to Law, he's not a legal Witness."

"Why is he not a legal Witness?" the judge asked shrewdly.

"My Lord, no Man can be allowed to be Witness in his own Case. He is a Party, my Lord, he can't be a Witness."

The judge saw no one in the witness box, but he pursued his advantage, saying, "The Man may be a Witness for the King, as in case of a Robbery on the Highway we always allow the Person robb'd is a good Witness."

The defendant, his eyes now fixed in terror on the witness box, moaned, "Nay, if you will allow him to be a good Witness, then I am a dead Man."

So far as the judge was concerned, a deceased witness was as good as a live one, and in this case even better. He told the accused man that his guilt was obvious and that he should confess his crime. The man burst into tears and made a full confession. He admitted that he had seen the ghost of the murdered man standing in the witness box. The ghost was baring his throat, which the prisoner had cut.

"THE BOATMAN WAITS"

Just as there are conscientious people who intervene on the side of fair play, even though they are not personally involved, some ghosts do the same thing and ask no credit for their good deeds. In one of the most fascinating cases of this kind, it seemed that a miracle had occurred to free a man unjustly accused of a crime. The ghostly voice never revealed its identity; it was merely content to use a living person as an instrument of justice.

In the early part of the 19th century, a young Cambridge undergraduate was on vacation in the town of Exmouth, on the river Exe in England. As he lay asleep in his hotel room one night, he heard a voice say, "Go down to the ferry." Since he hadn't the slightest intention of going down to the ferry, he ignored the command and went back to sleep. Once more the voice said, in an imperious tone, "Go down to the ferry," then added, "The boatman waits."

The young man lit a candle and looked around, but there was no one else in the room. He got back into bed and began to doze. Once again the voice said, "Go down to the ferry. The boatman waits."

Well, thought the young man, if the voice was going to keep this up all night, he might just as well go down to the ferry and see what it was all about. He got dressed and walked over to the dock. Although it was late, the boatman was still there, and he gave the college lad a cross look.

"Well, you have kept me waiting long enough tonight," said the boatman. "I've stopped here over an hour for you."

The young man had never before seen nor communicated in any way with this boatman. He asked the man what the devil he was talking about. The boatman insisted that earlier in the evening, the boy had told him he wanted to be taken across the river to the Starcross railroad station.

As the kind-hearted young man did not want to disappoint the boatman, he got into the boat and was rowed across. What next? He heard the voice again: "Exeter, Exeter. Go to Exeter."

He didn't want to go to Exeter, which offered nothing special in the way of diversion for a college student on a holiday, but he thought he might as well see it through. He took a train and arrived in Exeter at dawn, when the town had not yet come to life. He waited for further instructions from the voice, but it said nothing. The young man wondered whether his mind had been playing tricks on him.

He strolled around for awhile, then ate breakfast in a hotel. When he asked the waiter if there was anything exciting going on in town, the waiter said why not go down to the Assizes? There were sure to be some very interesting cases being tried—murders, pilferings, wife-beatings—a crime to suit every taste.

Having nothing better to do and by now having written off the voice, which seemed to have lost interest, the young man went to the Assizes. A murder trial was in session, and he made his way through the crowded courtroom and found a seat up in front.

The evidence was all on the side of the prosecution, yet the prisoner didn't look like a killer to the young student. The man, who was dressed in the work clothes of a carpenter, earnestly insisted that he was innocent, repeating that he could not have committed the crime because he was busy fixing a window on the day of the murder. Could he produce a witness, the judge asked? Alas, no, said the accused, but there was one man who could prove his innocence. Unfortunately, he did not know the man's name or where he could be reached.

The young student stared hard at the defendant, and his memory stirred. A few months before he had gone to visit a friend, who was not at home. While waiting for his host to return, he sat in the library and read a book. In this room a carpenter was repairing a window, and they spoke to each other. The young man had, in fact, taken out his notebook and jotted down bits of the conversation, using the carpenter's own stumpy pencil.

Now he took the notebook from his coat pocket and found that he had marked the very date of this visit—the day on which the now familiar figure in the dock was accused of having committed a murder. He gave evidence to the judge, and the defendant was acquitted.

This story appeared originally in *Strange Things Among Us,* by Captain Henry Spicer. The young man never did find out to whom the ghostly voice belonged, but it does prove that some ghosts are not only determined to see justice done but know just what steps will lead to the desired result.

A GHOST
CHANGES HIS WILL

There are all kinds of injustices in the world of living men, and no one knows this better than a ghost. The undeserving frequently reap rewards that should go to others who have worked hard or are next in line for an inheritance. Sometimes a man before his death wants his property disposed of in a certain way, but his instructions are ignored. As a ghost he must use all kinds of ingenious devices to get the attention of the living and make them understand what he had had in mind.

The famous story of Thomas Harris is an example, and so impressed was a member of the Maryland Council, before which the case was heard, that he took notes and published a detailed account of the trial. This account is now available in many libraries.

Thomas Harris, the councilman tells us, was taken ill while working in his farmyard one day in the latter part of the 18th century and died soon after. His will appointed his brother James as executor of the estate and stipulated that the property should be sold and the proceeds divided among his four children. Because the children were illegitimate, a technicality in the law prevented them from inheriting the land. James kept the money, and the children were left penniless.

Enter ghost of Thomas Harris. A close friend of Thomas, William Briggs, was riding near the cemetery one day on a horse that had belonged to Tom, when the horse suddenly stopped, trotted over to the fence, and neighed loudly. Briggs, who had been with Thomas when he died, was now amazed to see the dead man walking toward him, wearing the same blue coat he had usually worn when alive. As Harris came nearer, he suddenly veered off to the right and faded away.

Some time later, while Briggs was plowing his field, the ghost of Harris appeared again, still dressed in his blue coat. He walked along with Briggs for awhile but said nothing. Briggs' helper, John Bailey, came up and Thomas vanished.

While in bed one night Briggs saw a shadow on the wall and felt a body pressed against his. On another night he heard a loud groan that was exactly like the sound Harris had made when he died. Mrs. Briggs also heard the groan and commented about it to her husband. A couple of months later Harris appeared again and placed his hands on Briggs' shoulders, then faded away.

By now Briggs was pretty well shaken, and with good reason. Since Tom had been his friend, he couldn't understand why the ghost should play these macabre games with him. Harris' appearances did have a purpose, however, but for some reason known only to spirits, it took a good deal of maneuvering before he could get his message through.

Harris finally spoke, but not until he had startled his friend a few more times. One day, while Briggs and Bailey were stacking grain, Tom appeared by the fence, leaned over casually, and looked at Briggs. William stopped working, climbed over the fence, and the two old friends, one living and the other dead, took a stroll. Harris began talking in a low voice, but Briggs couldn't make out what he was saying. He asked Tom why he did not appear to his brother James instead of to him.

"Ask me no questions," said Tom enigmatically, then continued, "Ask my brother if he does not remember the conversation which took place between us on the east side of the wheat stacks the day I was taken with my death sickness. I wish all my property should be kept together by James until my children are of age. Then the whole should be sold and divided among them; not now. The children will be most needful of my property while they are minors, so I changed my will. You will see me again." Then Tom vanished.

Briggs told the story to James, who admitted that he had had such a conversation with Thomas. He promised to tell the authorities, but his wife, Mary, having had a taste of the money, didn't want to let go of it. When James died suddenly, the case was taken to court, and because Briggs was known as an honest man, his testimony was accepted, and the money was put in trust for the children.

In this case the court took seriously the notion that the ghost of Thomas Harris had written a new will and had appeared to William Briggs and told him about it. To the councilman who took notes at the trial, it was an "authentic account of the appearance of a ghost in court."

MEMBERSHIP REGISTRATION Fort Wayne Museum of Art — 1976-77

Mr./Mrs./Ms.

last _____ first _____ wife's first _____

Street & No. _____

City _____ State _____ Zip _____ Phone _____

Categories of Membership	Fees
Educator	$7.50
Junior (under 29)	10.00
General	15.00
Sustaining	25.00
Contributing	50.00
Patron	100.00
Life	1,000.00

Membership ☐ New ☐ Renewed

Museum Activities	Fees
Tues. Exploring Arts	$10.00
Wednesday Exploring Arts	12.00
Creative Cookery	8.00
Indoor Gardening	8.00

Amount Paid $ _____

I wish to charge this on my:

☐ Bank Americard: No. _____

☐ Master Charge No: _____

Signed _____

[IX]

GHOSTS
WHO MADE
HISTORY

There are compelling reasons why famous persons return as spirits, and the literature of ghostlore is filled with accounts of witnesses who have seen and heard them. Why do they come back? They are drawn irresistibly to the settings in which they were the chief characters in great dramas of the past. The ghosts of kings and queens, of prime ministers and presidents wander through historic structures such as Windsor Castle, the White House, the House of Commons, and palaces once ruled over by European monarchs, where they reenact the scenes of their triumphs and failures. The trauma of losing her head to the executioner binds Anne Boleyn to the Tower of London. The ghost of Marie Antoinette has been seen in front of the Petit Trianon in Versailles, reliving the days just before she was led to the guillotine.

The famous ghosts who are preoccupied with their memories are not unfriendly ghosts; they are merely oblivious to the mortals who see and hear them. Other famous ghosts are still concerned about the welfare of those who were once their subjects or their constituents. Queen Elizabeth was seen in Windsor Castle in 1926, presumably worried about a marriage of which she did not approve that had been arranged for the Prince of Wales. When a crisis faces the United States, the ghost of Abraham Lincoln is likely to appear and give silent encouragement to the occupants of the White House.

Washington, D.C., with its many historic buildings and rooms, is full of famous ghosts. Several of these old structures are being renovated, a fact that seems to discourage the spirits of those who once lived in them, but many are still untouched by demolition crews and are available for haunting by the ghosts of public figures who date back to the founding of the Republic. The Octagon House, so called because of its architectural design, was overrun with ghosts for decades after it served as a temporary dwelling for President Madison and his wife, Dolly. The Woodrow Wilson House on "S" St. is haunted by a ghost, but the attendant doesn't know for certain whether it is the restless spirit of our wartime President whose footsteps he hears.

The spirit of John Quincy Adams is said to roam through the old chamber of the House of Representatives. In the basement of the Capitol, an unidentified spirit walks back and forth, hands clasped behind him as he worries about some piece of legislation that may be forgotten today.

RESTLESS SPIRITS
IN THE
WHITE HOUSE

Every room in the White House is filled with memories, and many of them are haunted by past Presidents and First Ladies. Abe Lincoln paces through the East Room, where his body once lay in state, or stands thoughtfully at the window in the Oval Room facing Virginia. William Henry Harrison, who died after just one month in office, roamed through the attic before the White House was remodeled during Theodore Roosevelt's administration. Live Presidents come and go, but the spirits remain. They have been seen in the days of Grant, Garfield, Taft, Truman, and others.

Each dead President appears to be living once again through the trials of office, while each First Lady is once more the proprietress and hostess who makes sure that the daily life of the White House runs smoothly. While Dolly

Madison tends her garden or perhaps gives one of her celebrated parties, Abigail Adams moves through the long hall at daybreak, wearing her cape and a lace shawl. She passes through the double doors of the East Room, disappears, and reappears later hanging up her laundry there. The wife of John Adams was the first First Lady to occupy the White House, and when she moved into the as yet unfinished building, she was appalled because there was no place to dry clothes. She told the servants to hang the wash in the East Room, then known as the "audience room."

Possibly the only First Lady who has not returned in spirit to the White House is the straight-laced wife of Rutherford B. Hayes, called "Lemonade Lucy" because she would not allow liquor to be served. It may be that Dolly Madison and other more lively and permissive First Ladies don't want her there spoiling their fun.

Who has seen these famous friendly ghosts? Mostly the White House domestic staff—the butlers and maids, the janitors, the watchmen, even a barber who came regularly to shave the Chief Executive. Presidents and members of their staffs have either seen the ghosts or sensed them. Among those who have commented on or written about these famous spirits are Garfield, Lincoln, Theodore Roosevelt, and Truman. Mrs. Coolidge saw the ghost of Lincoln, while Eleanor Roosevelt said she often felt that Lincoln came into her sitting room, which had been his bedroom when he was in the White House.

Although the presence of George Washington has been sensed many times at Mount Vernon, he has not yet appeared at the White House, probably because he died before it became the seat of government. There is evidence that during his lifetime Washington professed a belief in ghosts. His friend Anthony Sherman wrote that Washington told him about a strange vision he had had at Valley Forge: the ghost of a very beautiful girl appeared there in 1777 and projected for him a picture of the perils that would threaten the new country in the next hundred years or more. The spirit warned that America would be in danger from other nations but would eventually triumph.

Possibly because our greatest crisis occurred during the Civil War, the ghost of Abraham Lincoln dominates the rooms and corridors of the White House. Although his most dramatic appearances are in wartime (he was often seen during Franklin D. Roosevelt's administration), he has appeared so many other times as to be considered a permanent if incorporeal occupant of the White House. He seems to favor the special room that is dedicated to his memory, the Lincoln Room, and was once observed sitting on the bed he had slept in when alive and taking off his shoes.

When Queen Wilhelmina of the Netherlands was a guest at the White House during Roosevelt's administration, she heard a knock on her bedroom door and saw the ghost of Lincoln standing there. Carl Sandburg, whose scholarly works rank high among the many biographies of Lincoln, once visited the White House and stood quietly at the window of the Oval Room on the second floor. Then he turned and said that this must be the room in which Lincoln had written certain letters reproduced in Sandburg's books. He had sensed Lincoln's presence.

It was well known among his contemporaries that Abe Lincoln had a mystical streak. He told an aide once that he believed the spirit of his dead son Willie was constantly with him. He had been reading a volume of poetry; putting the book aside, he said thoughtfully that he was certain he would see his boy again. The ghost of Willie also appeared to servants in the White House during Grant's administration.

Lincoln often held séances in the White House, especially when he was troubled by affairs of state. A reporter was present at one of the sessions, in April, 1863, and it was publicized in newspapers throughout the country. Although Lincoln gave serious attention to what the spirits told him, he could never resist making witty observations about the dead as well as the living. Charles E. Shockle was the medium on this occasion, and after going into a trance, he announced that an Indian spirit was present who wished to address the President.

"Well, sir," said Lincoln, "I should be happy to hear what his Indian Majesty has to say. We have recently had a visitation from our red brethren, and it was the only delegation, black, white, or blue, which did not volunteer some advice about the conduct of the war."

The medium then asked for paper and pencil, which were put on the table and covered with a handkerchief. When the paper was uncovered, there was writing on it, signed by Henry Knox, who had been the country's first Secretary of War. The spirit of Knox advised Lincoln to "make a bold front and fight the enemy. . . . Less note of preparation, less parade and policy talk, and more action."

Knox said that those in the spirit world who had served the nation were still concerned, particularly about the outcome of the Civil War. At one point Lincoln asked Knox "if it is within the scope of his ability to tell us when this rebellion will be put down." Knox replied that a group consisting of Washington, Lafayette, Wilberforce, and himself, with Napoleon sitting in, had been discussing this very point—but they could come to no consensus about the best course of action. This caused Lincoln to comment wryly that "opinions differ among the saints as well as among the sinners. They don't seem to understand running the machines among the celestials much better than we do. Their talk and advice sound very much like the talk of my cabinet. . . ."

Lincoln was assassinated on April 14, 1865. For many years after that, a phantom train appeared every April on the New York Central Railroad tracks in Albany, New York. This was the funeral train retracing the slow, melancholy journey that took the body of the 16th President from Washington to its last resting-place in Illinois. An item in the *Albany Evening Times* told how the track-walkers and section hands would sit along the track in the early evening of April 27, waiting for the train to come into view as it had in previous years.

At midnight the engine would appear, moving silently down the track with black streamers flowing from its sides and dark instruments playing a dirge. The ghost train would glide very quietly over a black carpet that seemed to cover the tracks, while ghost soldiers in Civil War uniforms trotted along, coffins on their backs. As it left the station, the train would become smaller and smaller, finally fading away. The railroad men would then check their watches and the station clock. Each timepiece had stopped when the train appeared and started once more when it faded from view.

The shock felt by the nation on April 14, 1865, took years to wear off, but the memory of Lincoln as a wise, witty, and compassionate man lives on. And, if we are to believe the testimony of countless persons who have seen him, Lincoln himself lives on in the White House, his benevolent spirit watching over the country and its people.

WANDERING GHOSTS
OF ROYALTY

The ghosts of kings and queens will not rest, especially if there were dramatic events in their public and private lives. In England the ghosts of Henry VIII, Richard III, George III, Queen Elizabeth, and many more still haunt Windsor Castle and Hampton Court. Anne Boleyn is seen everywhere in England but mostly in the Tower of London. She is usually accompanied by her faithful followers, those troubled souls who carried into the spirit world the burden of her unhappy ending. Often she is at the head of a procession of these souls inside the church in the Tower, moving down the aisle in an eerie light—a friendly ghost, bearing herself proudly once more as the young queen of all of England.

Although Anne and the other royal ghosts are peaceful spirits, they frequently scare the wits out of sentries and others who work or live in the castles. Anne is suspected of being the "tube ghost," who first appeared in 1817 when Edward L. Swifte, Keeper of the Crown Jewels, was having dinner with his family in the jewel house of the Tower. Swifte's wife called his attention to a figure in the shape of a glass tube floating between the ceiling and the table. The contents of this tubelike figure were a pale blue fluid. In more recent years, the tube ghost was seen again moving across the courtyard of the Tower of London, much to the consternation of a sentry there.

In 1926 a sergeant of the Sixtieth British Rifles, on guard in the Tower, saw another royal ghost. He tried to pin the apparition to the door with his bayonet, a tactic that is never successful with ghosts. The spirit immediately vanished, and the sergeant was taken into court and accused of being drunk, which he vehemently denied. A British princess once saw a royal ghost in the Tower, but she took it quite calmly. Not so her black cat, which squealed in terror, leaped out of a window, and broke his leg.

The two most frequent royal ghostly visitors at Windsor Castle are Charles I and Queen Elizabeth. Surprisingly, Elizabeth spends a good deal of her time in the library, probably reading the works of Shakespeare. In 1897, one of the Grenadier Guards saw her pass through the main reading room, dressed in black with black lace over her head and down past her shoulders. He assumed that she had gone into an inner room to work and asked an attendant who she was. The attendant, who had been asked this question many times before, replied casually that it must be Queen Elizabeth, a frequent visitor to the library.

There is evidence that Elizabeth regards herself as the all-time Queen Mother, watching over the affairs of England's living monarchs. In 1926 her ghost was seen pacing in the Saxon Tower of Windsor Castle, perturbed, so the theory went, by the possibility of a marriage between the Prince of Wales and Beatrice, the teenage daughter of Alfonso VIII of Spain. Perhaps Elizabeth was anxious that the young girl avoid the fate of Catherine of Aragon. A marriage had once been arranged between another Prince of Wales, Arthur, the older son of Henry VII, and Catherine, then the 16-year-old daughter of Ferdinand and Isabella of Castille. When Arthur died, Catherine became the first wife of his brother, Henry VIII, and a turbulent period followed in England's history.

Elizabeth was evidently successful in warding off the marriage of the 20th-century Prince to Beatrice. Whether she appeared again when Edward gave up his right to the British crown and married an American is not known. King Edward, having a mind of his own, probably would not have listened to his ghostly ancestor, imperious as Elizabeth could be.

Henry VIII let loose a whole batch of troubled spirits when he disposed of his many wives. Catherine of Aragon, his first wife, is frequently seen walking down a staircase in Hampton Court Palace, wearing black and carrying a lighted candle. Catherine Howard and Jane Seymour are regular visitors to Hampton Court. Anne Boleyn used to appear in the Tower of London the night before the anniversary of her execution and walk slowly around the scaffold. There is probably much unfinished business on the agenda of Henry's wives, and some day a thoughtful ghostologist may find a way to bring peace to their spirits.

Those who worked closely with royal figures are also driven to return to the scenes of their dramatic past. One of them is Sir Francis Drake, another Thomas à Becket, whose ghost appears in Canterbury Cathedral on one of the pillars of the crypt. Just as the contemporaries of Anne Boleyn join her in ghostly processions, the members of Marie Antoinette's court have materialized with her in a scene from the past. Two Victorian ladies on vacation in France in 1901 were wandering around the site of Louis XVI's court at Versailles when the modern setting miraculously changed, and the people around them appeared in the costumes of 1792. A lady sitting in front of the Petit Trianon looked very much like Marie Antoinette.

Throughout the continent of Europe, the seats of kings and queens and their dynasties hold memories, pleasant and sorrowful, that go back for many centuries. Each old palace is haunted by its particular ghost or ghosts. A spirit called the White Lady attached herself to the Hohenzollerns and appeared as a harbinger of death and other bad news for five hundred years after her own tragic death in the 14th century. Kaiser Wilhelm II at first refused to believe in the ghost, but she came to him one night while he was having a consultation with his advisors. The White Lady may have had a message which, if heeded, could have averted much suffering, but the Kaiser flew out of the room, regarding her as an evil omen rather than as a ghost with a warning service.

Three different kings saw the ghosts who haunted the Royal Palace at Stockholm—King Haakon of Norway, King Frederick of Denmark, and King Gustav of Sweden. The wife of Alexander the Second was said to haunt the winter palace at St. Petersburg. Isabella of Bourbon, wife of Philip IV of Spain, appeared three days after her death to a nun, Maria de Agreda. She was not only a friendly but also a repentant ghost, and she asked Maria to pray for her because she had been so vain of her beauty when alive.

A tender friendship between Empress Elizabeth of Austria and her cousin Ludwig II of Bavaria continued after death. Ludwig drowned himself in 1886 in the Lake of Starnberg, and his ghost came to Elizabeth many times. About a year after his death, the Empress was in bed one night when she heard the sound of lapping waves and felt as though she were drowning. Then the door opened and the ghost of Ludwig walked in, water dripping from his clothes. He came up to the bed, regarded Elizabeth sadly, and told her that she too would soon be a spirit. She died a few years later.

Perhaps the strangest of all royal ghosts was one that

confronted Catherine the Great of Russia. This haughty lady was proceeding into the throne room of her palace one day, accompanied by her pages-in-waiting and other attendants, when she stopped short and gaped at a remarkable tableau—a ghostly queen was being seated on the throne by ghostly attendants. The spirit queen was an exact duplicate of herself, her own ghost.

To the proud Catherine this was an affront that called for severe punishment, even if her own astral body was the culprit. She ordered her guard to fire upon the impostor. The bullets went through the throne, and the mirror behind the throne was shattered. Catherine then calmly sat down and began the day's business. Where the ghost went was never determined.

THE LITTLE CORPORAL RETURNS

While he was alive and the scourge of Europe, Napoleon was regarded by very few persons as a friendly soul. Nor would anyone believe that this soldier with a lust for conquest would give any of his time and attention to the spirit world. Yet Napoleon did commune with spirits, and there is evidence that he came back at least once as a friendly ghost.

The White Lady of the Hohenzollerns visited Napoleon one night while he was sleeping in the old palace in Berlin, perhaps to give him a warning. According to an account written by his bodyguard, Marshal Ney, Napoleon jumped out of bed and ran through the hall of the palace shouting that he had seen the ghost. A search through the house revealed no intruder, but at one point there was a loud crash. A painting of the White Lady had fallen to the floor.

Just as Kaiser Wilhelm refused to listen to the White Lady, so did Napoleon get away from her as fast as he could. Another ghost called the "Red Man," who had attached himself to Catherine de' Medici, also tried to give

Napoleon a friendly warning. Before the Emperor was about to set out on his ill-fated Russian campaign, the Red Man visited him in the Tuileries and strongly urged him not to go. Military leaders are notoriously headstrong, however, and will not listen to guardian ghosts. Napoleon ignored the Red Man's advice and came to grief in Russia.

When Napoleon was in captivity at St. Helena, he had plenty of time to think about spirits. General de Montholon, who was sent with him into exile, writes in his *History of the Captivity of Napoleon at St. Helena* that the ghost of Josephine once came to Napoleon. "I have seen my good Josephine," he told de Montholon. "She is not changed— still the same, full of devotion for me. She told me we were about to see each other again, never more to part. . . . Did you see her?"

On May 5, 1821, while Napoleon was in exile, his mother, Madame Bonaparte, was sitting in the drawing room of the Palazzo Bonaparte in Rome. On the floor below a strange-looking man appeared at the door and requested an audience with Madame. At first the hall porter would not admit him, as he had never seen the man before and no appointment had been made. The stranger, who wore a large cloak and a broad-brimmed hat drawn low over his face, insisted that he must see Madame Bonaparte at once—he had news of her son on the island of St. Helena.

The porter was doubtful; but he took the stranger upstairs to an anteroom, where another servant asked him his name and business. He replied that his message was so important it must be told to "La Signora Madre" herself. When Madame Bonaparte was informed, she sent word that she would see the stranger, and he was escorted into the drawing room. While the ladies-in-waiting were leaving the room, he held his cloak over his face and said nothing.

Finally, still covering his face, he said in a low dramatic voice, "Madame, the Emperor is freed from his sufferings. May the 5th, 1821—today!—he died. You will meet him again after some years." Then he retreated slowly, his hand still covering most of his face, and stepped out of the room, letting the portière fall behind him.

For a moment Madame Bonaparte remained in her chair, stunned. Her son was dead! But how could the stranger know? It would take months for news to travel that distance. And the man himself—she was sure she had seen him before.

Rousing herself, Madame Bonaparte rushed into the apartment beyond the drawing room, but it was empty. Then she hurried into the anteroom and asked a servant where the man had gone. The servant, whose business it was to sit all day in this room, replied: "Excellent Signora Madre, no one passed through. I have not left this place for a moment."

Madame Bonaparte ordered an immediate search throughout Rome, but the man was nowhere to be found. In the days that followed she spent long hours in her chair, thinking about her son and wondering who the stranger was and how he knew about Napoleon's death. Although she could not see his whole face, he seemed so familiar to her that she had been breathless throughout the interview. Could he possibly have been . . . ? Two and a half months later, Madame Bonaparte received news that her son had died at St. Helena—the date, May 5, 1821.

After that, Madame Bonaparte often spoke about the stranger to her lady-in-waiting, Madame de Sartonville. In the end she was certain it was the Emperor himself, for he had "the same figure, the same voice, the features, eyes, and commanding presence."

Was it the spirit of Napoleon? Madame Bonaparte thought so, and for the rest of her life she cherished the memory of this visit from her devoted son, who came to her incognito as a friendly ghost.

[X]

WISTFUL
LITERARY
GHOSTS

There are ghosts who enjoyed reading and writing when in their physical bodies and are drawn after death to literary surroundings. The spirit may be that of a man of letters such as Walt Whitman, Dante, or other authors who have been seen as ghosts, or merely a thoughtful soul of no particular eminence who seeks the company of books and writers as he did in life. The distinguishing quality of these souls is a gentleness of demeanor. They are ghosts who come and go quietly.

Sometimes a famous writer comes back to visit a friend, as Walt Whitman did when his friend Horace Traubel lay dying. Sometimes he wants to disclose that a manuscript of his lies undiscovered in a chest or closet. Dante allegedly visited his son Jacopo and told him where thirteen cantos missing from the *Divine Comedy* could be located. Often it is the living writer who sees the ghost of a non-literary person. Thackeray claimed that he had visitors from the spirit world, as did Madame de Staël, Tasso, and others. And there has been no more sensitive interaction between writer and book-loving ghost than between the living Nathaniel Hawthorne and the dead Dr. Harris.

Finally, of course, books themselves are the attraction for ghosts. Thousands of gentle souls must daily be roaming the corridors or passing by and through the bookshelves in public libraries or in someone's personal library, seen only by those who understand why ghosts would spend time in such unlikely places. Not the least of these spirits is that of Queen Elizabeth, a familiar figure in the library at Windsor Castle.

HAWTHORNE'S
GENTLE GHOST

The ghost who likes to read leaves the haunting of houses to his more extroverted fellow ghosts. He is generally quiet and unobtrusive, and he slips in and out of libraries unnoticed by any but the most finely tuned of living persons. Nathaniel Hawthorne saw one of these ghosts and wrote about him.

It was Hawthorne's custom to spend time each day in the reading room of the Atheneum, a library in Boston. This was an imposing structure, formerly a town residence, and the reading room was quite spacious, with groups of statuary at both ends. The most solid citizens of Boston did their reading and research here—lawyers, doctors, clergymen, philosophers, and merchants of the better class. In this atmosphere absolute silence prevailed. If anyone had spoken above a quiet whisper, he would have been severely reprimanded by the librarian.

Among those who came each day to the Atheneum was the elderly and highly respected Rev. Dr. Harris, a Unitarian minister, then in his eighties. Hawthorne knew Dr. Harris by sight but had never been introduced to him, and it would have been a breach of decorum to start a conversation with the old gentleman in the library. He had often passed Dr. Harris on the street and described him as "small, withered, infirm, but brisk, with snow-white hair, somewhat stooping figure, but remarkable alacrity of movement."

Each day, for months and years, Hawthorne would enter the reading room at noon, and the Rev. Harris never failed to be sitting quietly in his chair by the fire, reading the *Boston Post* or some other newspaper or magazine. When Hawthorne left later in the day, the clergyman would still be there, perhaps frowning over the editorials in the *Post*.

One evening, after coming from the library, where Dr. Harris had been as usual sitting and reading in his favorite chair, Hawthorne was told by a friend that the clergyman was dead.

"But he can't be," Hawthorne remonstrated. "I saw him at the Atheneum today."

The friend insisted that Harris had died and gave details of his demise. Hawthorne decided that he had been mistaken in thinking he had seen the minister. Dr. Harris could not be both dead and alive.

The next day Hawthorne entered the Atheneum at the noon hour and, in his own words, "As I opened the door of the reading room, I glanced toward the chair and spot where Dr. Harris usually sat, and there, to my astonishment, sat the gray, infirm figure of Dr. Harris, reading the newspaper."

He stared for a long time, but the vision of Dr. Harris did not go away. It struck Hawthorne that Dr. Harris could be reading his own death notice, printed in the morning *Post*. Certainly other persons in the library, many of them friends of the deceased, must have seen the notice, and some of them were planning to attend his funeral. Yet not a soul paid any attention to the quite solid figure sitting in the chair by the fire.

Or was he there? Hawthorne glanced over once more. If it wasn't Dr. Harris, the resemblance was certainly remarkable. The man in the chair looked and acted exactly like the real-life Dr. Harris, never once glancing at Hawthorne or the other occupants of the reading room, intent only on the news stories in the *Boston Post*. When Hawthorne left that day, Dr. Harris was still in his chair, still reading.

Every day after that, when Hawthorne entered the reading room, he glanced at the chair by the fire, and every day Dr. Harris was in his accustomed place. This went on for weeks, then months. It could be no trick of the imagination or play of evening lights, as it was always broad daylight when Hawthorne came in and when he left, and sunshine streamed through the tall windows of the reading room.

One day, to Hawthorne's surprise, Dr. Harris looked at him. The ghost lifted his spectacles and gazed steadily at the writer. What should I do now, thought Hawthorne? Should he speak to the ghost or wait for the other to make the first move? Hawthorne wanted very much to say something to Dr. Harris, but he knew that to disturb the tranquility of the reading room for any reason whatsoever was close to sacrilege. And if he explained to these proper Bostonians that he was addressing the ghost of Dr. Harris, his sanity certainly would have been in question. So Hawthorne said nothing.

Often after that, the ghost of Dr. Harris would lift his head from the newspaper in his hands, shove back his spectacles, and look at Hawthorne. It seemed to the latter that the expression in the ghost's eyes was one of disappointment and sadness. One day, as Hawthorne left the reading room in late afternoon, the sad eyes followed him to the door. The next day Dr. Harris was not in his chair, and Hawthorne never saw him again.

Generally we attract to ourselves the kind of ghost who appeals to our temperament and way of life. It is appropriate that Hawthorne's ghost should have been a reserved, studious lover of books and periodicals. Hawthorne never lost faith that the ghost was real. Writing about his experience years later, he declared that what he said was "the sober statement of a veritable fact."

THE GHOST
IN THE
BOOKSHELVES

If a librarian should die and find himself a ghost, what would be more natural than for him to return to his books?

This story begins back in 1880, when the librarian in an English hamlet died and a new man took his place. Nothing happened for four years, and if the ghost of the first librarian was back in his old surroundings during that time, his successor didn't know about it. This was just as well, because the new librarian was a nervous man, too apt to grab a gun when he heard a noise he could not account for. One cannot blame him completely, however, for he was a conscientious man who loved his books, and he knew there were many book thieves around.

One brisk March night in 1884 the librarian stayed at his desk later than usual. He planned to take the 11:05 train home and, looking at his watch, saw that he had better hurry if he wanted to get to the station on time. With a couple of books in one hand and a lamp in the other, he got up from the desk in his small office and walked out into the hall that led to the main library. Then he froze.

The lamp threw a light on the face of a man standing at the end of the connecting hall. The librarian hurried back to his office, opened the safe, and took out his revolver, then went back into the hall. The man had gone into the reading room with its many shelves of priceless volumes. The librarian ran into the main room, but it was dark and he could see no one. He swung the lamp around, then saw the face again, peering at him from behind one of the bookshelves.

"His head was bald and colorless," the librarian later told investigators from the Society for Psychical Research, "and the orbits of his eyes were very deep. He was an old man and his shoulders were very high." The librarian was puzzled because the man's body seemed to be in the bookcase, with his face outside. At first he was looking at some of the books, but suddenly—to the amazement of the librarian—he rotated out of the end of the bookcase, then walked with a shuffling gait into a small lavatory off the main room of the library.

Waving his revolver, the librarian ran into the lavatory, but no one was there. The window was closed and locked. If the intruder had climbed out, he would have had to jump ten feet into a skylight window below, and there would have been smashed glass. No one was on top of the skylight and the glass was unbroken.

The mystified librarian put his revolver back in the safe and went home. In fact, he returned home quite late, because he had missed his train and had to wait a long time for another one.

The next morning he told the story to a clergyman, who said, "Why, that's our old librarian, who died four years ago." The new librarian had never met his predecessor, and he was shown a picture of the dead man. The face was strikingly like that of the vanishing intruder. The man in the photo had no hair or eyebrows, having lost them in a gunpowder accident. The orbits of his eyes were very deep. And, said the clergyman, he had very high shoulders and walked with a peculiar shuffle.

There is no record of a return visit by the old librarian. Perhaps he did come back and the new librarian, understanding why he was there, allowed him to shuffle through the main reading room or, if he preferred, to rotate out of the shelves that held his beloved books.

THE BROWSING
GHOST

What do ghosts read when they visit libraries? They generally flit up and down the aisles or pass through bookshelves, as the old librarian in England did, but they are rarely seen looking at specific books. We do know that the ghost of Dr. Harris kept up with the news in Boston, and perhaps other ghosts, interested in current events, scan the daily papers or weekly and monthly magazines. Or they may thumb through ghost stories, real and fictitious, shuddering at accounts of macabre creatures who haunt graveyards, or reading with approval about the good deeds of friendly ghosts.

There was a ghost who haunted the old Astor library in New York City, and he left no doubt about his literary tastes. The Astor library was on Lafayette Place in downtown New York, and many writers of the mid-nineteenth century, among them Washington Irving, used to drop in to browse or chat with the librarians. There were some learned gentlemen on the Astor staff, including Dr. J. G. Cogswell and Daniel Willard Fiske, who later became a professor at Cornell University. In such a sophisticated atmosphere, a ghost should not have expected to be taken seriously.

Dr. Cogswell was in the library late one night, carrying a lighted candle and looking over the books in the upper galleries. He heard a slight movement and peered down at the west end of the south main gallery. A man was standing there reading a book. Since the library was closed for the night and all the doors locked, Dr. Cogswell wondered who he was and how he could have entered the building.

As he walked over to where the man was standing, the latter hastily put the book back on the shelf and vanished. The startled Dr. Cogswell stood for a moment to collect his scattered thoughts, then picked up the book the stranger had been reading. It was an old French folio edition of Nostradamus's *Predictions,* published in the 16th century.

Some time after that, again late at night, Dr. Cogswell saw the same ghost thumbing through the volume of Nostradamus. When the ghost vanished this time, Dr. Cogswell had no doubt he had seen a bona fide spirit. But whose spirit? Could it be Washington Irving, recently deceased, who had written about Rip Van Winkle and headless horsemen and therefore might be interested in the occult?

When the browsing ghost showed up a third time and picked the book off the shelf, Dr. Cogswell tiptoed up and got a closer look. It was neither Irving nor any of the other writers of the past who had been familiar figures in the Astor, but a physician from down the block who had died a few weeks before. Cogswell reported his experience to the trustees of the library, who told him he had been seeing things and sent him off to the country for a rest.

There is a link between the Astor ghost and the ghost of Washington Irving. Before his death in 1859, Irving sauntered into the library one day and asked Fiske and another staff member, Frank H. Norton, if they would witness a will he had just written. After Irving's death his nephew, Pierre Irving, visited Norton in the library and told him that the spirit of his uncle had returned to his country home, Sunnyside.

Pierre Irving and his two daughters had been sitting in the front room of Sunnyside, talking, when one of the young ladies stood up and exclaimed, "Why, there's uncle!" They all saw the ghost of Washington Irving come through the front, dressed as they remembered him, walk through the parlor, and go into the Sunnyside library, where he had done his writing when alive. When they went inside, the room was empty.

Perhaps writers do not come back to haunt public libraries because they often have their own well-stocked personal libraries, where they return to read or work on a manuscript. Washington Irving might have left a book or short story unfinished when he died and come back to complete his writing. As for the Astor ghost, he had probably died unexpectedly while reading Nostradamus, and his first order of business as a ghost would have been to resume reading where he had left off. After three nocturnal visits to the upper galleries, he must have finally finished the book, because he didn't appear in the Astor library again.

The story of the Astor ghost was written up in the New York newspapers of the 1860s and recounted by Frank Norton in a letter to *The Nation,* which appeared in the issue of April 20, 1911.

GHOST OF
A POET

The friendly ghost of the poet Walt Whitman was seen by not just one person but two, and both saw him at the same time. One of them was also a poet.

Horace Traubel was not only a writer of verse but Walt Whitman's close friend and biographer. Traubel outlived Whitman by more than twenty years but in September, 1919, he lay dying in a town in Ontario, Canada. With him was Lt. Col. L. Moore Cosgrave. Two days before Traubel finally expired, Col. Cosgrave was sitting at his bedside. About 3 A.M. he noticed that Traubel was staring in fascination at something over his bed. Cosgrave looked up.

The two men saw a point of light appear that slowly spread into a mist and finally contracted into a human face. The features became distinct, and the two men recognized the face of Walt Whitman. Whitman's spirit-body materialized and stood beside the bed wearing clothes that were familiar to Traubel—a rough tweed jacket and an old felt hat. Whitman had his right hand in his pocket, and he smiled down at Traubel.

"There is Walt!" Traubel exclaimed.

The ghost of Whitman nodded, then passed through the bed toward Cosgrave, who got the impression that Whitman touched his hand. He said later that it felt like a low electric charge. The ghost then smiled again at Traubel and faded away.

Walter F. Prince, an investigator for the American Society for Psychical Research, wrote about the vision of Whitman in his book, *Noted Witnesses for Psychic Occurrences*. After Traubel's death, Cosgrave sent two letters about his experience to Dr. Prince, and the case was also written up in the Proceedings of the Society for Psychical Research.

Recently the American Society for Psychical Research did a survey of nurses and doctors to find out how many dying persons saw spirits at their bedside and what the mental condition of the patients was at the time. One of the striking features of this survey was that most of the terminal patients were quite rational when they reported their visions. The Whitman case is doubly impressive because two persons, both of them of sound mind, saw the ghost of the poet and reported it in detail to investigators.

[XI]

A MEDLEY
OF MUSICAL
GHOSTS

In the 1890s there was a magazine for violinists and music teachers called *The Violin Times*. The editor was startled one day when he received a check in the mail from a new subscriber in Idaho, who wrote that he had been told about the magazine by a woman in the spirit world. The ghost had been alive fifty years before, had been a violinist, and was now teaching the man who wrote the letter how to play the violin. The budding musician said he was making good progress.

When musicians return as ghosts, they usually signify their presence by singing or playing an instrument. The moody ghost who haunts an old house called Dunleith in Natchez, Mississippi, plays a harp and sings sad melodies. Organists have come back to play organs, pianists play pianos, there have been guitar-playing ghosts, and even drummers, the loudest of the lot. While Caesar was hesitating at the Rubicon, a musical ghost tried to lure him to the other side with reed-pipe music. When this didn't work, the impatient shade seized a trumpet from the grasp of one of the military and made such a racket with it that Caesar hurried across the river, probably to get away from the noise.

Violinists, amateur or professional, often take their instruments into the spirit world with them. A Houston public library is haunted by a janitor who lived in the basement before his death. When his day's work was done, he would fetch his fiddle and stroll through the empty rooms, playing until the early hours of the morning.

After he died, he continued this practice but was discreet enough to wait until the library was closed, as he had done during his lifetime.

Often music is used to send a symbolic message. Camille Flammarion, the astronomer who investigated ghosts, tells about a piano that played by itself whenever there was a death in the family. In most cases, of course, the purpose of the music is to let friends and relatives know that the one who has died still lives on in the spirit world and still plays or sings. Since music is a spiritual language, however, much of it comes in the form of ethereal singing, often by inspiring choruses, but the identity of the performers is unknown.

A ghost who appeared to Mozart may or may not have been a musician himself, but he had a message for the composer. This ghost told Mozart to write a requiem and came back many times to goad him into finishing it. When it was completed, Mozart died, and the requiem was played at his own funeral.

THE GHOST AND
THE CHOIRMASTER

The choirmaster had a problem. It was already Friday afternoon and he had not yet chosen music for the Sunday service at St. Luke's Church. He went into the library of his home, and after much hesitation selected two "Te Deums," which he took upstairs to his study. Spreading the music sheets on the desk, he stared at both pieces and frowned. The "Te Deum" he favored required the services of a second tenor, but he was not sure that a good one was available in all of San Francisco.

The choirmaster, Mr. Reeves, lay down on the couch to mull over the tenor problem. Why were tenors so difficult to find and then so unreliable when you did locate them? Often they failed to show up for rehearsal and occasionally did not even make it to the service itself.

Perhaps their instability of character had something to do with the range and timbre of the voice. It was a theory worth investigating. Basses, for example, were just the opposite. Mr. Reeves rarely had trouble with basses.

Take that Mr. Russell, for example—always on time for rehearsal, always in his place for the Sunday service, always pleasant and smiling. Moreover, Mr. Russell had a rich, deep voice that was a pleasure to hear. Come to think of it, Russell had promised to visit him this weekend.

Hearing a slight noise, the choirmaster looked up. There, standing at the door, was the very person he had been thinking of—Edwin Russell. The bass singer had one hand on his brow and the other was holding a sheet of music. Smiling, Mr. Reeves got up from the couch and went over to the door, extending his hand in welcome.

Mr. Russell and the music disappeared.

In the parlor below, two ladies and a gentleman named Mr. Sprague heard the choirmaster shout, "Oh, my God!" The ladies, his sister and niece, rushed up the stairs, followed by Mr. Sprague. They found Reeves sitting on the stairs in his shirtsleeves, muttering, "I have just seen Mr. Russell." The two ladies looked at each other, and the niece said gently, "Mr. Russell is dead."

Russell had indeed passed away that morning following a cerebral hemorrhage, and the rector of St. Luke's had sent over Mr. Sprague with the sad news and with a request that Mr. Reeves choose music for the funeral.

Rarely does a ghost appear without a motive, and usually it is a friendly one. The clue to the behavior of the spirit who appeared in the choirmaster's study may be found in the character of the living Mr. Russell. Always conscientious and now concerned because he could not attend either the rehearsal or the service, he probably wanted to convey this information to the choirmaster and return the music, which he would no longer need.

The incident occurred in San Francisco in 1890 and was reported in a daily newspaper and investigated by members of the Society for Psychical Research.

WHICH GHOST
PLAYED THE
CHURCH ORGAN?

It was the year 1883. The body of Henry Ditton–Newman lay in state in the chapel of St. John's Church. Henry had died suddenly from an attack of pleurisy, and it was a shock to the members of the church, who liked the pleasant young organist. As they filed past his casket, they recalled the previous four years and what a pleasure it had been to come to Sunday service and hear the rolling chords from the pipe organ. Where could they find another organist who would play with the same skill and enthusiasm?

As if in answer, the organ began to play, filling the chapel with thundering chords and arpeggios, just as Henry had done. This time, however, no one was sitting at the organ. It was playing by itself.

St. John's Church is in Torquay, on the coast of Devon in England. For almost eighty years after Henry's death, the organ gave impromptu recitals under ghostly fingers. Live organists came and went, new vicars replaced the old ones, parishioners were born and died—still the organ continued to play by itself. Every device was used to discourage the ghost of Henry. Holy water was sprinkled on the organ seat, the clergyman tried exorcism, the instrument was even sent out and rebuilt. But Henry played on.

Every organist at St. John's sensed Henry's presence at the keyboard, and they felt that at times he was playing right along with them. Musicians are a touchy lot and don't like competition, even from a ghost. One unnerved organist resigned and another, Frederick Fea, wrote to the Bishop of Exeter and asked him to do something about kicking the ghost out of the church.

Each vicar had his own theory as to why Henry kept playing the organ. One recalled that he had written music when he was alive and thought he kept coming back to complete his unfinished compositions. It didn't occur to any of the vicars, or to anyone else, for that matter, that Henry loved the organ and particularly enjoyed playing the great pipe organ that was the pride of St. John's Church.

Not that the vicars were unhappy with Henry's presence. The sudden booming of the organ, especially at night when the church was empty and quiet, startled them, but his playing had a friendly, joyful quality that uplifted the spirits of all who heard it. Even the Rev. Patrick Ferguson Davie, vicar in 1945, who once chased the ghost downstairs with a riding whip, said he felt that Henry was a friendly spirit. It's just that vicars usually don't care to share their churches with ghosts, even friendly ones.

Henry was still playing in 1956, and by this time he was a famous ghost and was written up in English and American newspapers. No one doubted that it was the ghost of Henry Ditton–Newman at the manuals of the organ. But then something peculiar happened.

Up to this time there had always been a feeling of lightheartedness when the ghost was present, and this was reflected in the music that came out of the organ. Now a strange depression replaced the former mood and the music became doleful, even gloomy, losing its earlier brightness. A pall hung over the rooms of the church, particularly over the third floor. The choral society practiced on this floor, and once they were frightened when a weird noise came out of the organ and a ghost suddenly appeared, then vanished.

The vicar, now the Rev. Anthony T. Rouse, wondered why the mood of the ghost had changed. Was something bothering him? In 1958 the Rev. Rouse went to London and consulted with a medium. While in trance, she came up with the surprising news that it wasn't Henry Ditton–Newman who was playing the organ, but another ghost!

In 1956 the church organist had committed suicide but had not received a proper burial, or so the ghost thought. His body had been left outside the church while the funeral service was held, and the ghost didn't think this was right. While alive, this organist had lived on the top floor of the vicarage, where the sense of depression was most acutely felt after his death.

The Rev. Rouse placated the spirit of the second organist by sprinkling holy water over his grave, praying, and reciting a psalm. After this was done, in 1959, the strange feeling of sadness lifted from the church, and from that day on no ghost ever played the organ again.

Which ghost played the organ at St. John's Church? Since the second organist had died in 1956, it must have been Henry Ditton–Newman who was there in the 1883–1956 period, but he was evidently ousted from the organ seat in that year by the gloomy ghost of the later organist. Since Henry did not return after 1959, it must be assumed that he finally finished his compositions or that he has found an organ in the spirit world he can play to his soul's content.

THE GHOST WHO
HAD RHYTHM

If it were not for the Marquis de Mirville, well known in France for his work on pneumatology (the doctrine of spiritual beings), the world might never have heard about the mysterious goings-on at the Cideville Parsonage in the middle of the last century. It was de Mirville who collected all the documents in the case from the legal records.

The affair started with the usual knockings in one of the upper rooms of the parsonage. After patiently enduring this for about a week, the curate, Monsieur l'Abbé Tinel, decided to address the invisible carpenter.

"Strike louder!" challenged the curate, and he was instantly sorry he had spoken, for his ears were assailed by a frightful din. After that the hammering was twice as loud.

A few days later one of the two young boys who were staying with the curate spoke to the ghost: "Beat time to the tune of 'Maitre Corbeau.'" The ghost immediately pounded out the rhythm of this tune, and the two boys, following the beat closely, said that not one mistake was made.

A visiting curate, Auguste Huet, also talked to the ghost and devised a game. Huet tapped his finger on the edge of the table, saying, "Strike as many blows as there are letters in my name." Four blows were struck at that very spot. Switching to music, the visiting curate asked the ghost to beat time to a tune called "Au clair de la lune." The ghost did so—without losing a beat.

The ghost of Cideville Parsonage was about as active a spirit as a ghostologist could find. In addition to his musical talent, he was quite a magician and put on many a show for visitors. The curate's dogs, strolling about the rectory one day, were amazed to find themselves lifted to the ceiling and then gently lowered to the floor. Chairs would often rise in a group and hang in the air.

When the Mayor came over to see what it was all about, the ghost entertained him by making tongs leap from the fireplace and land in the middle of the room, then repeated this trick with a shovel. For another curate, Monsieur Leroux, the ghost caused a piece of bread to move across the table by itself, then drop quietly to the floor. When Monsieur Dufour, a land agent, was present, a table walked around the room on its own power.

The Marquis de Mirville finally heard about the ghost of Cideville Parsonage and came forty-two miles to investigate. He asked the ghost how many letters there were in his name; eight blows were given for de Mirville's last name and five for his given name—Jules. There were five raps for the name of his eldest child, Aline, and seven for that of another child, Blanche.

De Mirville then tested the ghost's musicianship, and for the first time the ghost stumbled. After beating time perfectly to several tunes, he hesitated when asked for a selection from "William Tell." Someone hummed the melody for the ghost, who then beat out the rhythm without an error.

Even after all these remarkable performances, many people still did not believe in the ghost, and they said that a living person was responsible. The finger of suspicion was even pointed at the curate, as honest a man as could be found in France. De Mirville defended him, saying that he would be "greatly astonished if any person in this neighborhood could entertain such an opinion."

Then it was whispered that the two young boys were the culprits, since the mysterious movement of objects and other such phenomena are often associated with the presence of young children. There was not a shred of evidence, however, that the children by themselves could cause the disturbance. Since a suspect had to be found, a shepherd who had bragged that he knew something of the black arts was accused of practicing sorcery against the children. Thorel, the shepherd, was fired from his job, as no decent man wants a sorcerer working for him.

Meanwhile the whole thing was giving l'Abbé Tinel a violent headache. The curate was a peace-loving man who not only couldn't sleep nights because the ghost kept beating time; he resented seeing his parsonage turned into a theater, and he resented even more the accusations hurled at him and his young guests. When the curate accidentally ran into the shepherd, neither was in the mood for a friendly talk. Thorel threatened to hit the curate, and the curate, a man of spirit, whacked the shepherd with his cane.

Thorel promptly brought suit for damages against the curate, charging that he was unjustly accused of causing the disturbances at Cideville. The trial took place at Yirville in January, 1851, and the courtroom was packed with spectators who had heard about the ghost. There were thirty-four witnesses in court, each with a different story about the redoubtable ghost of Cideville. The judge finally decided against the plaintiff on the grounds that the shepherd, who had a weakness for bragging, had claimed that he did in fact have an influence on the Cideville ghost.

It is true that after the children left the parsonage the disturbances ceased, but that doesn't prove they had anything to do with it. The simplest answer is that a fun-loving ghost with an ear for music was having his kicks at the expense of the serious-minded citizens of Cideville.

Ghost hunters are delighted that the trial was held, because it gave de Mirville a chance to examine the many depositions given by the witnesses and collect voluminous material about this famous ghost. Later, Robert Dale Owen wrote up the story in *Footfalls on the Boundary of Another World.*

A STRANGE
NEW YEAR'S EVE PARTY

It was once an ivy-covered white house surrounded by trees, an 18th-century home with graceful arches in the gothic style. Today the trees remain but the house is gone, except for the original gateposts and, here and there, a few stones.

Yet every year, on December 31st, the guests return for their annual New Year's Eve celebration, among them distinguished gentlemen from the Georgian period, wearing their frilled shirts and white silk stockings. On this night the house rises once more, the guests are greeted at the door by their gracious hostess, and soon there is music and dancing. Through the windows one can hear the sweet strains of waltzes and minuets and catch glimpses of ladies swishing by in their billowy gowns.

Of course, there is no absolute proof that the house materializes and that the party takes place every New Year's Eve as it did back in the 1700s. We have to take the word of a young lady and her friends of a more recent era, who went back twice and witnessed the re-enactment of an old scene. On the first occasion, five persons in the girl's party saw the bright lights from the house shining through the trees and heard a lovely soprano voice sing to the accompaniment of a harpsichord.

All five saw and heard the same thing, but the young lady wanted to be sure. Two years later she came back again on New Year's Eve, with a friend who had not been there before. There were the old gateposts, the trees, and some stones, and nothing more. And then, as they waited nearby, a miracle occurred. The house slowly rose in the clearing surrounded by the trees, the lights came on, coaches rolled up to the gates, and men and women dismounted and walked up the path to the house.

Once more the music began. They heard the rich tones of the tenors, then the clear, light voices of the sopranos. They heard duets, part songs, delicate airs played by a flute. Often there was cheering and applause.

As the bells of midnight tolled in the New Year, a magnificent tenor voice sang, "God rest you merrie gentlemen," and the jolly expression of goodwill was repeated in chorus by the guests—"God rest you merrie gentlemen!"

Now, while dogs barked and the porch lights went on, the door of the house opened, and the ladies and gentlemen of another era slowly filed out and got into their coaches, which clattered off down the road, becoming smaller and smaller and then disappearing.

Gradually the lights in the house dimmed until there was darkness, the murmuring of voices died away into silence, and the house itself faded until only the trees and the stumps of old gateposts were left.

[XII]

SOCIABLE GHOSTS
IN THE ORIENT

A Japanese professor, Dr. Chuta Ito, writing in an old issue of *Japan Magazine,* declared that a ghost is "likely to partake of characteristics of people among whom he appears." Ghosts in oriental countries, although they are pretty much like ghosts in other parts of the world, have a certain charm they have absorbed from their culture and taken into the spirit world. One example is Mr. Bu of Burma, who only went about his ghostly chores on Tuesdays and Saturdays, vacationing with his spirit friends the rest of the week. Another is the one-legged ghost described later in this chapter. This friendly ghost, in common with his Japanese countrymen, was the soul of courtesy, and his conversation with the landlord should be a model for communication between living and non-living persons.

The life of a ghost is made rather easier in oriental countries because most people there thoroughly believe in them. There is a town in Japan where three days of the year are set aside for entertaining visitors from the next world. During the "Feast of Lanterns" in September, the people of the town put on their holiday clothes and assemble in their living rooms to await their invisible guests. When the spirits arrive, there is much eating and drinking, and when they depart on the third night, a procession of the living carries their boats to the sea, where they will row back to the spirit land.

To the Chinese, the dead are not very far away. If the relatives of a Chinese gentleman are deceased, he will simply say they are not present. (At least this was true before the Mao-worshippers took over.) Each family has an ancestral shrine where souls of dead relatives may visit, and here the living offer food and clothing for the departed, also paper money to make purchases in the spirit world. In an *Asia* magazine article dated May, 1931, Rodney Gilbert, a one-time China correspondent for the *New York Herald Tribune,* observed that "The ghost story in China, if it is a current one, is not regarded as creepy fiction but as an item of local news."

The Chinese are fond of stories depicting romances between girl ghosts and young men. Because the physical body is considered a vital part of the spirit entity, the ghosts in these stories are as solid and lifelike as the living. The writer P'u Sung-ling collected presumably true stories from the people of 17th-century China and told the charming tale of the young student Tao Wang-san, whose cottage was so hot and uncomfortable that he went to live and study in a haunted house. While he was sitting one night writing a theme on "The Non-Existence of Ghosts," the spirits of two beautiful girls came in and began to tease him. At first he refused to acknowledge their presence, for it would have been contrary to his scholarly ideas. Finally he came to enjoy their company and even showed them how to copy notes from his books.

In addition to ghosts who are native to oriental countries, there are many Englishmen who had lived so long in India that after death they chose to return there rather than go back to the mother country. One of Calcutta's most persistent ghosts is Warren Hastings, who lived there in the 18th century. Hastings, while alive, missed some important documents and advertised for them in the *Calcutta Gazette* of Sept. 6, 1787. He died without finding them, however, and now, every evening his spirit drives up in a coach, gets off in front of the Hastings House, and carefully searches the house for a black wooden bureau in which the documents had been placed.

THE GHOST WITH TWO SERVANTS

Nighttime in the Punjab, when the moon is full, is a propitious time for the appearance of ghosts, particularly in the mountain regions, where they look very solid in the clear night air. Back in 1854, a ghost on horseback journeyed up a road that wound around a mountain to visit an English soldier, accompanied by two Indian servants who were also ghosts.

The soldier, General Barter, was at that time a subaltern attached to the 75th regiment, and he lived in a house built on a spur that jutted out from the side of the mountain. It was not easy to find his house, even for a ghost. To get there the ghost had to travel up the only road that came from the base of the mountain until he reached the very top, seven thousand feet above sea level. Then the ghost descended a bridle path that went past the house three hundred yards below and ended in a precipice. A footpath led from the bridle path to the house.

It was on this footpath that subaltern Barter was standing one night, when his two dogs began to whimper in fright. He heard the sound of horses' hoofs and saw a tall stovepipe hat appear around the sharp bend in the road above him. The man wearing the hat was on a dark-brown horse, and on each side of the animal a *syce* (groom) was walking and holding the bridle close to the bit with one hand while the other hand supported the rider.

The horseman appeared to be paying a formal call, because he was dressed in a dinner jacket and white waistcoat. What jolted his host, however, was that he was sitting stiff as a corpse in the saddle, holding the reins loosely as his arms drooped, and staring straight ahead as if seeing nothing, his face deathly pale in the moonlight.

"Quon hai?" called Barter. ("Who is it?")

There was no answer. The party halted at the footpath, but the dogs hung back, whimpering.

"What the devil do you want?" demanded Barter.

The rider took a firmer grasp on the bridle reins and looked down at the subaltern, who recognized an old army lieutenant friend he had not seen for some time. But the man's appearance had altered shockingly. His face was puffed up and surrounded by an unfamiliar fringe of hair, while his body had grown very stout.

Barter peered up at the man's face, and chills ran down his spine. It was the face of a dead man—white and expressionless. Suddenly the rider jerked the reins, and the horse wheeled around and trotted down the road toward the precipice, followed by the *syces*. Barter ran up the footpath after them but stumbled and fell, scratching his hands on some stones. When he looked up, the rider and his horse and servants had disappeared. He walked up the bridle path in both directions, but there was no sign of his strange visitors.

The following morning the subaltern spoke to a friend who had been in the lieutenant's regiment. The friend confirmed that the lieutenant had died and also that he had become very bloated before death and had allowed his hair to grow around his face. His horse, a dark-brown pony with a black mane and tail, had been killed earlier during a reckless ride down the side of a mountain.

The ghostly rider with the horse and two servants was also heard by Barter's wife and Hindu servant. Each night for many nights there came the sound of a horse riding down the path toward the house. The horse's hoofs would stop, but when the servant opened the door, no one would be there.

Barter learned later that the house he lived in had been built by the dead man. Once, when Barter's Hindu servant was standing on the footpath, the phantom horse and rider swept by him like a strong wind. The Hindu shuddered, pointed to the house, and called it a "Shaitan ka ghur hai"—a devil's house.

The case of the ghost with two servants was investigated by the Society for Psychical Research. General Barter described his experience in a letter to the Society in 1888, and letters from his wife and others involved gave corroborating testimony.

Were the lieutenant and his grooms and horse merely coming to pay a friendly call on Barter and his wife? Or were they drawn back to the house because it was filled with memories of their life on the earth plane? Perhaps the ghost and his retinue did indeed come back as sociable spirits but were discouraged by the whimpering of the dogs and by Barter's hostile attitude.

THE SOLDIER WHO DIDN'T SALUTE

Englishmen are known throughout the world for their good manners, and their courtesy and regard for proper conduct are generally carried over into military service. An English soldier on duty in the colonies always wore a clean and carefully pressed uniform and was respectful to his superiors. If he forgot to salute, a shudder would go through the officer corps. The senior captain of the 74th Highlanders, a regiment in India during the 19th century, once got the surprise of his life when a young private took his leave without saluting. Even more shocking was that he entered the captain's presence wearing white pajamas.

At the time, the Highlanders were in service southwest of Hyderabad in the state of Sholapore, and the captain was sitting in his tent going over his papers. One of the sidewalls of the tent was open to admit a breeze, but it was one of those hot, sticky days when nothing stirred. The captain was quite uncomfortable and somewhat testy, but he went on with his work.

Suddenly, without seeming to enter, a young man stood before him. The captain looked up, annoyed. It was bad enough to be interrupted in this rude way, but what made it worse was that the lad was dressed in the white clothes of a hospital patient. He recognized the soldier as a private in his regiment.

"What the devil—" started the captain, putting down his pen.

"Please, sir," the young man interrupted in an urgent voice, "I wish you would kindly have my arrears of pay sent home to my mother. Please take down the address."

The captain should have reprimanded the young man

and told him to see the sergeant with his request. Instead, he found himself taking a pad of paper out of his desk drawer and writing down the address in England that the soldier gave him. The young man watched him write, then without a word withdrew past the open sidewall.

The captain, as if in a trance, stared at the address he had written down. Then the awesome realization came to him that the soldier had not saluted. And he, the senior captain of the 74th Highlanders, had taken orders from his brash visitor and made no protest. He called in his orderly and brusquely told him to fetch the sergeant. Belated discipline was better than no discipline at all.

The sergeant came in, saluted smartly, and stood at attention. Why, demanded the captain, had that private been permitted to burst into his tent in such an irregular manner?

The sergeant stared at the captain for a moment, then said, "Did you know, sir, that the man was buried this morning? He died in the hospital yesterday."

"But he just gave me his mother's address." The captain showed the address he had written on his pad. The sergeant looked relieved.

"Well, that does solve a problem, sir. We have just auctioned off the private's belongings, but we did not know where to send the proceeds. There was no address in our registry."

The money brought in from the auction was sent to the young man's mother, and she wrote back that she had been grateful to receive it, as she was in poor circumstances. As for the captain, when he returned to England years later and told the story of the private who didn't salute him, he added that in this case the young man could be forgiven.

MR. BU OF BURMA

The family and the servants were in a quandary. What should be done about Mr. Bu? He wasn't even an authentic

Burmese ghost because he came from Japan. As a Japanese soldier, he had hanged himself from a tree in the Rangoon compound and thereafter haunted the water tower a few yards away. The Burmese had enough of their own native spirits to worry about without having to deal with ghosts from other countries. Ogres, vampires, and other troublesome creatures could be soothed with tempting Burmese dishes, but what would you give a Japanese ghost—sukiyaki?

The servants were afraid of Mr. Bu, especially on Tuesdays and Saturdays, when he banged loudly on the water tower and made them pull the covers over their heads. Their quarters, in the rear of the yard and well back from the main house, were uncomfortably close to the tower. Whenever their American employers, Mr. and Mrs. Allen, were away for the night, the nannies would sleep in the house up front, one eye open to watch for Mr. Bu in case he decided to come down from the tower.

The only Burmese who really understood Mr. Bu was Sariti, the gardener, but for a long time he said nothing, just worked in the garden under the hot sun, wearing his loincloth and sandals as he cut the grass with his *dah* (curved knife). Gardeners in Burma are the lowest of the low, well beneath the nannies and other servants in status, and Sariti usually knew his place and made no complaints.

When the Allens took over the compound in 1963, they knew nothing about Mr. Bu. Lee Allen was an architect who had come to Burma with his family in 1961 to help build a university in Rangoon. Anne Allen, like most other Americans, didn't believe in ghosts. College-trained in anthropology, she planned to bring up her two daughters, four-year-old Cathleen and Maureen, the baby, in the rationalist tradition of the western world. The first house the family rented in Rangoon had no ghost problem, but the trouble started when they moved to the new compound two years later.

The Allens thought it odd when the servants grumbled, considering that the new quarters were much more comfortable. The main dwelling in front was a ranch-style *pukka* house with three bedrooms, quite modern with three air conditioners to fight off the oppressive Burmese heat. In the back were the servants' quarters—a long, motel-style house occupied by Salvaraj, the cook; Gna Nora and Gna Dwe Yin, the two nannies who watched over the Allen children; and Ma Ti Mya, another nanny.

Ma Ti Mya didn't take care of the children; her job was to do the washing. But she was by far the most striking of the nannies—a good-looking young woman who flounced about wearing an *ainjyi,* a see-through nylon blouse. Ma Ti Mya was quite outspoken and aggressive, always sure of herself. It was she who, in November, 1963, marched determinedly into the front house, followed by the other servants, and demanded that Mr. Bu be sent away.

Anne Allen was alone with her children at the time. Who, she asked, was Mr. Bu? Ma Ti Mya, gesturing and speaking in her loud, clear voice, told a story that was well known to most Burmese in Rangoon. Mr. Bu had been haunting the water tower since 1945, and each Tuesday and Saturday he could be observed sitting there and hitting it throughout the night.

"You can actually see him?" asked the incredulous Anne.

Americans don't understand. Of course you couldn't always see him clearly, Ma explained, but there was very definitely a glow on the tower. When one of the men climbed to the top of the tower, the glow would disappear, because ghosts can move very quickly.

"But if he only comes on Tuesdays and Saturdays," said Anne, "where does he go the other nights?"

The servants had various theories. Gna Nora thought he only worked part time and spent the rest of the week on vacation with his fellow ghosts, wherever they were. Gna Dwe Yin believed that he went to other water towers and haunted them. Little Cathleen Allen, who had been listening open-mouthed to the story, spoke up and asked if Mr. Bu took Sundays off, but none of the servants could answer that.

It was true that Mr. Bu never bothered anybody, and the worst that could happen was that the servants would be awakened on the nights he did his banging. But you never knew when he would climb down and get nasty. After all, he was a foreign ghost and therefore unpredictable.

All this talk made Ma Ti Mya very impatient, and she said that Mr. Bu simply had to go, that was all there was to it. It was very simple to get rid of him. Just call in the *pongyi,* the Buddhist monk. He would go back to the water tower, put up an offering, and yell "Twa! Twa!" And Mr. Bu would go away.

The other servants agreed that this was what had to be done. Anne was about to call the *pongyi,* but at this point Sariti came into the house noiselessly on his slim, sun-baked legs. Holding his *dah* in his right hand, he said in a quiet voice that he preferred they didn't call in the *pongyi.* Ma Ti Mya turned on him wrathfully, her dark eyes blazing and her ample bosom heaving in anger, and gave him a tongue-lashing. Not only wasn't it his place to speak at all, but why was he defending the foreign ghost, Mr. Bu?

Because, said Sariti patiently in his low voice, he liked Mr. Bu. It would be an act of discourtesy to call in the *pongyi,* even if Mr. Bu was a foreigner. After all, he had remained in Burma all these years when he could have gone back to Japan and haunted a water tower there, and this could only be a compliment to the Burmese. It would be extremely inhospitable to send him away.

Besides, Sariti continued, lifting up his *dah* for emphasis, Mr. Bu had been living back on the water tower for many years, far longer than the human beings who now inhabited the compound. Never, said Sariti, had he known a gentler and better behaved ghost. Had Mr. Bu, demanded the gardener, ever hurt any of them? Mr. Bu was Sariti's friend, and he wanted the ghost to stay.

The others saw the logic of Sariti's argument, all except Ma Ti Mya, who with loud talk and bluster tried to override the quiet-spoken gardener. Anne decided in favor of Mr. Bu—the *pongyi* would not be called in. The servants left, still grumbling, and Sariti went back to work in the garden and watch over his banana and papaya trees. He was never known to give any opinions after that except about his work. And Mr. Bu stayed.

The story of Mr. Bu was told to me by Lee and Anne Allen, with excited comments thrown in by their eldest daughter, Cathleen. There is a sequel. When the Allen family returned to America in 1965, Mr. Bu came along— at least Cathleen, now six, and three-year-old Maureen insisted they saw him in the elevator of the high-rise building in New York where the Allens were living.

Later, when the family bought a home in Bethesda, Maryland, Mr. Bu followed and settled in the basement. When I visited the Allens in 1969, Maureen told me that she had often seen him down there. It may be that he joined the family out of gratitude because they did not call the *pongyi,* or that he was tired of the water tower and decided to try a lower-level haunting for a change; or perhaps he just wanted to travel and see the world.

In any event, Mr. Bu was a welcome guest and a special favorite of Maureen's, who was proud of the fact that no other home in the community had a ghost in the basement. And just as Sariti had said, Mr. Bu was a friendly, well-behaved ghost, one of the nicest that could be found in any part of the world, east or west.

THE GHOST
WHO CAME
THROUGH THE WALL

Although a Chinese spirit has the same freedom of movement enjoyed by ghosts in the rest of the world, he is still concerned about his physical body, and any discomfort that the sleeping body suffers is felt by the freely moving soul. Rodney Gilbert, in his article in *Asia* magazine, described a Manchu ghost whose dead body suffered such indignities at the hands of the living that she came back nightly to petition for relief.

A very large house in Peking was empty for many years because the tenants claimed it was haunted. A man from Shanghai who was not familiar with the situation rented the house, much to the delight of the townspeople, who didn't care much for "southerners" and liked to see them humiliated. For awhile nothing happened—until the man went away for a few days and left his wife alone. When he returned, he found her living in the gatehouse, afraid to go back into the main house.

The wife explained that each night as she was about to retire on the *kang* (bed), the ghost of a young lady would wriggle through a crack in the corner of the room. First her hand would appear, then a Manchu headdress, then her head and face. The ghost would then moan softly, causing the wife to pick up her clothes and fly out of the room and into the gatehouse, where the distraught servants would join her.

The more practical husband, knowing the enmity of the townspeople toward him, suspected that his neighbors were playing a trick, and he made ready for them. That night his wife lay down as usual on the *kang,* while he waited with a sword in the next room. At the usual time there was a slight hissing sound, and the mist-like ghost oozed through the crack and shaped herself into the young woman with the Manchu headdress. The man ran in and hacked at the head with his sword, whereupon the ghost vanished. But on the floor lay part of a centuries-old Manchu headdress.

The next day the husband took the headdress to the police and explained what had happened, declaring that he wanted to break his lease and move out of the house. The landlord had to cancel the lease, but he asked the man to show him the exact spot in the wall through which the ghost had entered. He then called in workmen, who excavated under the spot. Many feet below the wall and under the foundation, they found an old coffin and in it a corpse dressed in a Manchu costume. Part of the head-dress had been sliced off.

The house had once been owned by a Manchu family, and the landlord located their descendants in another part of town. From hearing their story and examining old records, he learned that two hundred years before, mar-tial law had been declared and the city gates closed for a time. During this period the dead could not be buried, and their relatives had improvised burial grounds. A young woman in the Manchu family had died and was buried in a corner of the courtyard. Later the house had been rebuilt so that the wall of one bedroom was directly over the grave. The coffin was crushed by the pressure.

According to Chinese tradition, a spirit has three souls. One is the "grave soul," which is attached to the body and stays with it at death. The "grave soul" of the young lady, affected by the discomfort of the body, had come back each night to tell her story to the tenants. Since the living are very obtuse in these matters, the distressed ghost was never able to get her message through.

The landlord had the corpse removed and placed in another coffin, which was then buried where it belonged—in the family graveyard of the original Manchu owners. After that, there was no more trouble in the house, and the ghost of the young lady was relieved of a great burden as she went about her business in the spirit world.

THE
ONE-LEGGED
GHOST

One reason owners of haunted houses don't like to tell about their ghosts is the fear that their property will go down in value. This has been true throughout history. Pliny the Younger, a Roman statesman and writer, mentioned it when he described a haunted house in Athens. In Chicago an ordinance was passed in 1912 stating that houses known to have ghosts must be assessed at a lower rate. While I was ghost-hunting, a lady in an east-coast town refused to give me details about her haunted spinning wheel because she thought she would be unable to sell her house.

This attitude is unfair to the ghost. Very few ghosts will haunt a house longer than is necessary for their purposes, and all it takes to make them cease and desist is a little kindness and understanding about their problems. Play psychiatrist to your ghost and more often than not he will go away. It is also true that many ghosts come back to a house because it was theirs at one time, and they are just as interested as the present owner in maintaining the value of the property. One ghost, who had a sense of fair play and was disgusted with the neglect of his house after he died, appeared to a lady about to buy the house and warned her that the plumbing was bad.

In the Orient, landlords appreciate the ghost's side of it and are willing to meet spirits halfway. The owner of the Peking house haunted by the young lady in the Manchu headdress very sensibly made an investigation and discovered what was troubling her. Another case in which a landlord showed good sense occurred in a haunted house in Japan.

In this house, an unusually noisy ghost kept disturbing tenants, but instead of establishing rapport with him, they all moved out. The landlord, rather than bemoan his fate or apply for a lower assessment, decided on a different approach. He went to the empty house one night, sat in the hallway, and waited.

Soon he heard a very peculiar sound inside the house, as though someone were jumping around on one leg. After each jump there would be a pause, then the leg would hit the floor again with such a thud that the windows rattled. Presently a ghost with his left leg missing came hopping through the door on his one leg, putting his hand against the wall for support. Two or three times he lost his balance and fell to the floor with a crash. The last time the ghost just lay there and looked up pleadingly at the landlord.

The landlord inquired solicitously what was wrong, and the ghost explained that he had been a soldier who died in battle when his leg was shot off. The reason he came back night after night, hopping painfully on one leg and continually losing his balance, was that the missing leg was buried under the house. He apologized for making a disturbance and frightening the tenants, but added that if it were possible for him to have his leg back, he would go away and not return.

The landlord then fetched a shovel and went outside and to the back of the house. He had to walk very slowly because the ghost made it in hops, grabbing the landlord's shoulder for support. Finally the ghost pointed to the spot where the carnal leg had been buried. The landlord began to dig, and presently a mist arose from the spot and shaped itself into a man's leg. This spirit leg then drifted over to the stump of the ghost's leg and joined itself to the spirit body.

The ghost was now able to walk about like a normal ghost, and he thanked the landlord for his kindness. After that he didn't come back and the landlord prospered, for his apartments were never empty.

BE KIND TO
YOUR GHOST

In the New York offices of the American Society for Psychical Research, a letter tacked to the bulletin board reads:

> "We have a unique problem and at the outset we want to state that we are normal, intelligent people not in need of medical care, as we are both of the medical profession. Last March we purchased an older type of framehouse in a better than average neighborhood. Our problem —the house is haunted. We are both very upset at this ordeal. The lady ghost is a tiny, prune-faced female that constantly pulls my covers down on all my beds. Then she giggles and shuffles off, crying a dreadful, heart-sobbing cry. . . ."

The writer asks for help in getting rid of the ghost, but perhaps it is the prune-faced female and others in her halfway world who are more desperately in need of help. This type of ghost, whose behavior seems irrational to living persons, may only be trying to get their attention— just as disturbed children do mischievous things to alert parents to their problems. If this book has one main theme, it is that you should be kind to your ghost, and you will be rewarded with his gratitude and very likely his friendship.

The reader may recall that Count Hamon turned a noisy, scary spirit into a quiet, docile one who became the Count's friend and wanted to live with him in his new home. The Count's technique for treating ghosts is much more effective than that of the nervous librarian or the impulsive Captain Marryat discussed in this chapter, who grabbed their revolvers first and asked questions afterward. The one-legged ghost in Japan whose disability was responsible for the racket he made is another case in point, and if the landlord hadn't shown more understanding than his tenants, the handicapped ghost might still be hopping around at night, crashing to the floor or falling against the wall as he searched for his missing leg.

There are four true stories in this chapter about ghosts who needed help. In two of them, the living persons were far from kind to the unfortunate spirits, and it caused nothing but trouble in both ghostly and material worlds. In the last two stories, the tavern-keeper and the philosopher did help the distressed spirits, to the satisfaction of everyone concerned.

THE
BULLET-PROOF
GHOST

Captain Frederick Marryat was a man to reckon with, as his admiring daughter Florence, herself a psychic and ghost-hunter, admitted in her biography of him. A well-known writer of novels about the sea, the Captain was born in 1792 and became a leading figure in the English community where he lived. He was a man who would take no nonsense from anyone, neither human being nor ghost.

At the time Florence Marryat writes about, the Captain was a magistrate, and if there was one thing that got his gall, it was the young poachers who stole game from the properties of distinguished lords and ladies in the community. The Captain would have shot one of these upstarts on sight if he could have caught him in the act.

Therefore, when Captain Marryat's friends the baronet and his lady moved into Raynham Hall, he wanted to be sure they enjoyed their house and grounds and were not bothered by intruders. The baronet went to great pains to redecorate the mansion and make it a gathering place for the best people from both London and the surrounding country.

No sooner did the guests arrive, however, when word went around that the house was haunted and the servants were giving notice. As the domestics filed out, carrying their suitcases, they explained that the "Brown Lady" was scaring them half to death, appearing as she did on the stairs, then passing through the wall without bothering to walk down. The guests soon followed them—reluctantly, because they liked the leisurely country life and the hospitality of the kindly baronet. Soon only the baronet and his wife and two nephews were left in the large mansion.

Captain Marryat knew better—the ghost bit was just a decoy, and the damned poachers were trying to empty the house so they could raid it and the grounds at will. The Captain took his revolver, inserted a bullet, and announced that he would not only spend the night at Raynham but would put to rout the so-called "Brown Lady" and reveal her for the impostor she undoubtedly was.

As the Captain walked resolutely through the rooms of the mansion, he turned to look at a portrait that hung on one of the walls. It was the Brown Lady, or rather a picture of an old inhabitant of Raynham thought to be the ghost. She was wearing a brown satin dress with yellow trimmings and a ruff about her neck. Very pretty and genteel she looked in the picture. Captain Marryat snorted and went up to his room.

He stayed in the house for three nights, sleeping each night with the revolver under his pillow. The first two nights nothing happened, and the Captain wondered if the young scamps who were playing this ghost trick were lying low until he left. In that case, he said grimly, he would remain until he had met and dealt with this "ghost."

On the third night the Captain was getting ready to retire, when the baronet's nephews came to his room and asked him to look at a new gun they had just received from London. The Captain, wearing only a shirt and trousers, went to their room and examined the gun. Coming back into the corridor, he saw what looked like the light from a lamp moving toward him. As the light drew nearer, he recognized the Brown Lady of the portrait he had seen below.

The Captain was at first nonplussed, as he was a proper man but at that moment improperly dressed. Then the pure cheek of it struck him. What the devil was this ghost doing in the house, anyway? As if in answer, the Brown Lady smiled, but to the Captain that smile was a fiendish grin. He fired his revolver.

We who are familiar with ghosts and have seen what happened when General Jackson's "ghost-layer" shot at the Bell Witch, could have told Captain Marryat that he had wasted both his temper and his bullet. The ghost vanished, of course, perhaps offended by this display of violence. The bullet passed through the outer door of a room and embedded itself in the wall beyond.

After that, no one had to convince the Captain that a real ghost or certainly something devilishly mysterious was haunting Raynham Hall. If he was embarrassed by the incident, it was not for long, as the Captain was a proud man and not one to readily admit error. The people of the town, knowing what was good for them, were careful never to mention the Brown Lady in his presence.

Still, it is a pity that the Captain didn't hold a séance or get a clergyman to soothe the spirit of the Brown Lady, or at least try to talk to her himself. He might have found out what was troubling her, and they might even have become friends.

THE GHOST
IN THE
VIOLET DRESS

It must be admitted that ghost behavior is not always easy to understand. Knocks on the wall, scratches on the door, moans and wails in the middle of the night are a bit too much for timid souls like the vicar of this story, not to mention the unsettling habit ghosts have of suddenly being there one moment and gone the next. Still, it is the business of vicars to keep in touch not only with this world but also the next, and the foibles of ghosts should disconcert them no more than those of their parishioners.

The vicar of Ratherby Church often preached about the next world from his pulpit, but he believed that spirits should stay where they belonged and not come bothering those still in the flesh. Ratherby Church is in England, and Elliott O'Donnell wrote in the *Occult Review* about the peculiar happenings there in the early part of the century.

Vicar Bodkin, after a particularly difficult day attending to the duties of his parish, came into the vestry one evening ready for a well-earned rest. Pulling off his boots and wiping his perspiring brow (it was a very hot day in July), he was annoyed to see an old lady sitting there. Not only was it rude and tactless of her to come into the vestry without being announced; the vicar was further offended by her flamboyant dress. She wore a poke bonnet and a garish, violet-colored petticoat.

"What can I do for you, Madame?" asked the vicar stiffly.

The old lady did not reply; she just lifted her dress and pointed at one foot. Puzzled, the vicar adjusted his glasses and peered. She had on a patent-leather shoe with a polished silver buckle. Then she pointed at the other foot, which was in a violet stocking but no shoe. As the vicar stared, she disappeared.

Vicar Bodkin fell back in his chair, trembling. Had he been seeing things? He was not a drinking man, so it couldn't be that. Perhaps he had been working too hard, perhaps, it being a hot day, the light had been playing tricks.

Ten days went by. Each night when the vicar walked exhausted into the vestry, he half expected to see the woman with the violet petticoat and one shoe reappear.

Often he would look nervously over his shoulder, but no one was there. He began to relax once more.

On the tenth day, while the evening service was in progress, he saw her again—standing near the pulpit, wearing that repulsive violet dress and pointing at her shoeless foot. The rattled vicar picked up a box of matches and threw it at her, and she disappeared. Naturally, those in the church were astonished at what the vicar had done, since none of them could see the old lady. The vicar had turned pale and was muttering to himself. Members of the congregation took him home and told him to get a good night's rest.

When the ghost appeared a third time to the vicar, still pointing at the foot without a shoe, he merely closed his eyes and prayed until she melted away.

Elliott O'Donnell later led an investigation into the mystery of the old lady and discovered that she had been killed when she had fallen down a quarry. One shoe had slipped off her foot at the time, and she was later buried with just the other one. After the missing shoe was located, she did not appear in her ghost form again, and the members of the congregation were happy to see that Vicar Bodkin was once more his old, unperturbed self.

Had he been kind to his ghost in the first place, however, the vicar would not only have spared himself a great deal of anguish but would have brought peace to a disturbed spirit.

THE GHOST
IN THE TAVERN

Among the favorite haunts of ghosts are inns and hotels, possibly because some dramatic events, such as death itself, occur when one is traveling. Old Salem, a section of what is now Winston-Salem in North Carolina, boasts of a famous tavern once visited by a gentleman who returned as a ghost because of the courtesy shown him by the landlord.

Salem's reputation as a hospitable community began in 1766, when it was founded by Moravians from Pennsylvania. This religious group built a tavern in 1772 and instructed the landlord to show his guests "kindness and cordiality, but not to encourage them to be intemperate." Later, in 1784, a private tavern was built, the celebrated Salem Tavern, and it was here that the ghost appeared in the early 18th century.

Salem Tavern had already achieved a kind of fame when George Washington slept there in 1791. It was a typical hostelry of that time, with the restaurant and bar in front, the sleeping rooms upstairs, and a small office for the tavern-keeper at the rear of the first floor. One cold winter night, while the landlord was in his office looking over his menus for the following day, there came a faint knock on the door. He opened it and a man fell in from the hall, obviously very ill.

The tavern-keeper, a kindly man, sent for a doctor while a slave helped the man to an upstairs room. The stranger was asked his name but was so deathly ill he could only mumble an unintelligible answer. In due course the doctor came, gave the man some medicine, but told the tavern-keeper privately that he didn't think the patient would survive. Soon the stranger went into a coma and died.

There was nothing to identify the dead man—no initials or name anywhere on the saddlebag and no marks on his clothes. After he was buried, business went on as usual in the tavern, but strange noises began to be heard. This upset the maids and affected their work, as the presence of ghosts usually does. One night a slave dropped a tray of food and said in a trembling voice that someone was following him. No one was there, at least no living person.

Another time—at night, of course, when the scariest things happen—a maid ran into the landlord's office and cried hysterically that there was something in the hall. The landlord went out to look, and this time there was no doubt that a ghost was present. First there was a scraping sound on the floor, then a form materialized.

"Please tell my brother I have died," said the ghost, and he gave the landlord both his name and the name and address of his brother in Texas.

The tavern-keeper, instead of going into a panic just because a ghost was talking to him, calmly took down the two names and the address and assured the ghost that he would take care of the matter. He sat down that very night and wrote a letter to the brother in Texas, telling how the stranger had come into the tavern and giving a physical description of the deceased.

In time an answer came from Texas. Yes, the dead man was the brother of the Texan, and the description fitted him perfectly. Following instructions, the landlord sent the saddlebag to Texas.

The proprietor of Salem Tavern showed kindness twice, first to the living man who needed help, then to the ghost of the man, who could find no other way to communicate with his brother.

THE PHILOSOPHER
AND THE GHOST

The hero of this story is the Greek philosopher Athenodorus, who was able to help a ghost in need because he kept his equilibrium and did not fly out of his house at the first sound of clanking chains. Pliny the Younger, a Roman statesman and writer, wrote about the incident, and he thought Athenodorus conducted himself very well in the affair.

According to Pliny, there was in Athens a very spacious and comfortable house with many rooms that should have been a joy to live in—but no one would live in it. Every tenant who rented a room moved in and right out again after the first night, and each one told the same story. In the dead of night there would come a far-off sound like the clanging of metal, and this sound would gradually grow louder and noisier until it could be heard at the very door of the bedroom. Then the ghost of an old man would appear, "meagre and squalid, with a long beard and bristling hair, rattling the gyvves on his feet and hands." One night of this was enough for any Greek.

The landlord of the house was distressed because an empty house brought in no income. He posted a notice, stating that the house was to be let or sold, and gave a very low price in either case. Athenodorus, a Stoic and therefore not easily perturbed, saw the notice and wondered why the rent was so cheap for such desirable quarters. He made inquiries and heard about the ghost with the long beard. Since philosophers don't make much money, however, he could not afford to pass up this bargain, and he signed a lease for the house.

The first day he moved in, Athenodorus had a couch brought to the front part of the house and a lamp placed on the table along with his pen and tablets of papyrus. Then he instructed the servants to go to bed. Throughout the night he sat at the table writing on the tablets whatever it is a philosopher writes while he waits nervously for a ghost to arrive.

For a few hours nothing happened, as most ghosts like to build up suspense. Then, as his informants had warned, he heard the faint clanging sound of metal against metal that gradually grew louder and more frightening. Athenodorus kept on writing, perhaps a bit shakily. The clanging came near the door of his room, then into the room itself. Athenodorus put down his pen, looked around and full into the face of the ghost, who beckoned with his finger.

The philosopher must have been in the middle of writing a sentence, because he indicated that the ghost should wait, then turned back to the table to finish his thought. This ghost was not going to be put off, however, and he rattled his chains noisily over the head of the philosopher, enough to end all composition for the night. Again the ghost beckoned with his finger, then turned toward the door. Athenodorus picked up his lamp and followed the apparition, who went clanging out of the house and into the courtyard. The ghost paused for a moment on one spot, then melted away.

Athenodorus marked the spot with a handful of grass and leaves. Then he went back to his room, had a good night's rest, and late the next morning told the magistrates what had happened, suggesting that they order the spot to be dug up. They did so and found a heap of bones and chains just like those the ghost had been dragging. The bones were given a decent burial, and the house was haunted no more.

[XIV]

OFFBEAT
FRIENDLY
GHOSTS

Then there are the slightly off-center ghosts, the individualists who don't follow the rules laid down in books on ghost behavior. They are friendly, too, but their style is different from that of the conventional kind of ghost. Just like the free souls among the living, they are the nonconformists of the spirit world.

An example is the ghost who temporarily wanders away from a healthy physical body. Often the person in the body is not aware that his ghost-self has gone off on an adventure, called an OOB (out-of-body) experience by parapsychologists. Although most of the ghosts in this book are at-time-of-death or after-death spirits, I have included a famous OOB case—the ghost who went northwest.

Each of the other offbeat friendly spirits in this chapter has a unique style of ghosting—the "head" of the house, the odd couple of ghosts, the peeking ghost, the whistlers, the ghost who got lost, and last—but first, in order of appearance—the Abbé Peytou, who found life in the spirit unendurable without his snuffbox.

THE GHOST
AND THE SNUFFBOX

Chances are that few people have ever heard of the Abbé Peytou, curé of the village of Sentenac in France, yet he must rank high in the annals of offbeat ghosts. When the curé died early in the 19th century, the villagers of Sentenac were genuinely sorry. He had been a modest, God-fearing man whose only vice, if it could be called that, was a penchant for snuff.

A few days after the funeral, it was whispered that the ghost of the curé had returned. Each night, it was said, he was heard walking about the rectory, moving chairs from one room to the next as had been his habit when alive, and repeatedly opening and closing the snuffbox. The illiterate villagers of Sentenac all believed with their simple faith that the spirit of the curé had come back. All of them, that is, except the only two educated men in the village.

Messieurs Antoine Eycheinne and Baptiste Galy looked at each other with a knowing smile and remarked on the ignorance of the untutored, who swallowed the wildest tales without question. Antoine and Baptiste had studied mathematics and logic and knew a thing or two. It was up to them, the town sophisticates, to prove once and for all that ghosts did not exist. The curé had been a good man, they would grant him that, but where he had gone there were no more snuffboxes. If the gullible villagers had heard noises in the rectory, it had to be burglars.

Monsieur Eycheinne got his rifle, while Monsieur Galy found a hatchet, and the two men marched resolutely to the rectory, determined to camp there until the ghost appeared and then expose it as a fraud. They settled themselves in the kitchen, lit a good fire, and eyed each other bravely in the light cast by the flickering flames. They waited.

Suddenly there was a noise in the room above them—the scraping sound of a chair being moved across the floor. Antoine raised his rifle and pointed it at the ceiling, while Baptiste's grip tightened over the handle of his hatchet. After a brief pause, they heard footsteps in the hall above, then a slow clumping down the stairs. The two men tiptoed to the door, Antoine leveling his gun in the direction of the sound, while Baptiste raised his hatchet over his head.

Closer and closer the footsteps came, reached the door of the kitchen, then stopped. Now the ghost, or pseudo-ghost, whatever it was, clumped off toward the drawing room. A moment later they heard the sound of a box opening and closing, then a hearty sneeze. The box opened and closed again, followed by a second, even heartier sneeze. Then there was a long silence.

Breathing heavily, Antoine opened the kitchen door and advanced toward the drawing room, his rifle pointing ahead of him, while Baptiste was right behind him, his hatchet still held over his head. No one was in the drawing room, and the snuffbox rested on the mantelpiece. They climbed the stairs and looked around. No one was in the bedroom above the kitchen. They searched the whole house—every room, every closet. Each object was in place, and the ghost had disappeared.

Baptiste put down his hatchet and said, "Well, Antoine, what do you think?"

"Well, Baptiste," Antoine answered, scratching his chin with the muzzle of his rifle, "it is to our credit, at least, that we have not unthinkingly accepted the preposterous story that the ghost of the Abbé Peytou has returned. Unlike the other villagers, we have made a careful investigation in a scientific manner to see for ourselves." He paused, then added emphatically, "My friend, no living person is making this disturbance, it is the dead. It is Monsieur Peytou; it is his step and his way of taking snuff that we heard. We can now sleep in peace."

The late curé was also seen at dawn outside the church. A young lady of Sentenac, while taking her donkey to the mountain for a load of wood, saw him walking in the garden, reading a prayer book. She thought at first it was the new curé, but shortly after that she saw the live curé in front of the church. He said he had not been in the garden; he had just finished mass.

Ghostologists are indebted for this case to a schoolmaster who interviewed the elders of the village and sent a report to Adolphe d'Assier, of the Bordeaux Academy of Sciences. Monsieur d'Assier, who investigated 19th-century ghosts, published the story in his *Posthumous Humanity*.

THE GHOST
WHO GOT LOST

It has been generally assumed that a ghost knows his way around; that if, for example, he wants to visit a great-granddaughter somewhere in South Africa, all he has to do is fly right over to the exact spot where she is at the moment. This is not true of all ghosts. There are stories about ghosts who have gone for a friendly visit to a living person and wound up on the other side of town, scaring perfect strangers. Perhaps there are absent-minded ghosts just as there are vague people.

Adolphe d'Assier, a ghostologist of the last century, told about a ghost who got lost aboard a ship. An English officer who was taking a cruise on this ship was getting undressed in his cabin one evening when the door opened and an elderly gentleman looked in. The officer had never seen him before and wondered how he could have come aboard, since the vessel had been on the ocean for several weeks. The stranger stared at him for a moment, then shook his head from side to side and closed the door. The curious officer got dressed and went on deck. He saw the man go from cabin to cabin, opening each door and looking in, then shaking his head and going on to the next one. While the officer was following him, he suddenly disappeared.

The astonished officer found the captain of the ship and told him the story. "It appeared to me," said the officer, "that he was searching for someone. Just before he vanished, his expression was very sad." The officer described the man's appearance and clothes, and the captain said it reminded him of his father, whom the officer had never seen.

When the ship docked in England, the captain went to his home and was told that his father had died. While in a coma, corresponding in time to the appearance of the ghost, the delirious man had cried: "Whence, think you, I have come? Well, I have crossed the sea. I have visited the vessel of my son. I have made the rounds of the cabins. I opened them all, and I did not see him in any of them."

Which brings to mind another story about a ghost who set out to visit a relative and couldn't find her. Ghosts are very sensitive to both the physical and psychological environment, and any change in a house they are used to visiting may disturb and confuse them. If a ghost comes to see you, don't shift the furniture around too much, as they feel more comfortable in familiar surroundings. If you should move to a new apartment or house, be sure to notify your ghost, otherwise he or she may have trouble finding you.

A story told to me by a young lady from the West Indies illustrates this point. The young lady's grandmother, Rosa, lived for quite awhile on the first floor of a two-story frame house in Jamaica. Every morning at 5 A.M., the spirit of Rosa's mother would come up to the back porch and call "Rosa! Rosa!" Rosa listened but never answered, as she knew the ghost merely wanted to send a friendly greeting.

Just outside the house was a *yabbah*, a bowl-like object covered with a board which is used to keep water cool. Early each morning, when the spirit came to the door, she knew she was in the right place because the *yabbah* was always there.

After living many years in this house, Rosa moved to another one that was completely different in every way from her former dwelling. The other house was old; this one was new. Rosa had been on the first floor in the old house; in the new one she lived in a back room on the second floor. And there was no *yabbah* in front of the door.

For many months Rosa failed to hear the voice of her mother. Then one night, as she lay in bed half awake, she heard her mother say, in a plaintive voice, "Rosa, where have you been? I've been looking for you." The voice seemed to come from far away.

Again the next night she heard the voice of her mother say, "Where are you? Where are you?" One night the voice cried out in great distress, "I can't find you. I can't find you."

The young lady who told me this story wasn't sure whether her great-grandmother ever did find her grandmother's new home. Rosa did not quite know what to tell her mother. It is not customary to give a ghost directions: Go down this road, turn to the left, and so forth. If the ghost couldn't find her way to the new house, there must have been something in the physical arrangement that threw her off.

I suspect that a *yabbah* placed in front of the door would have made the difference.

THE GHOST
GOES NORTHWEST

The ship, bound west for New Brunswick, was sailing in a southerly direction. The first mate was sitting in his cabin, calculating latitude and longitude, and he could see the captain in his stateroom on the other side of the stairway, writing something on a slate. He called out his figures to the captain, but the latter, hunched over his desk, did not reply.

The first mate was puzzled because the other cabin was only a few feet away. He called out again, but again there was no answer. The first mate rose and walked past the stairway that descended from the deck and looked into the other cabin. The man writing on the slate glanced up and fixed him with a steady gaze. The first mate's blood froze; it was not the captain but a complete stranger.

He hurried up the stairway and found the captain on deck.

"Sir, who is sitting at your desk?"

"No one, Mr. Bruce."

"But there is, sir. There's a stranger at your desk writing on your slate."

"You must be dreaming, Mr. Bruce," the captain replied calmly. "No one on this ship would venture into my cabin without orders. And it can't be a stranger, because we are already six weeks out of Liverpool."

"But, sir, I distinctly saw him sitting in your armchair and writing."

"Well," said the captain, "let's look into this."

Together they descended the staircase, but there was no one in the captain's cabin.

"Well now, Mr. Bruce, I am sure you were dreaming. Do you see anyone here?"

"The slateboard, sir. There's writing on it."

The captain picked the slate off his desk and read the words: *Steer to the northwest.*

"What kind of trick is this, Mr. Bruce?" the captain thundered. "If you are playing a joke on me, you will pay heavily for it."

Bruce protested his innocence, and as he had always been a sober man attentive to his duties, the captain was inclined to believe him. Nevertheless, he asked Bruce to write the words *Steer to the northwest* on another slateboard. The handwritings did not match.

Each member of the crew was then called in to write the same words—the second mate, the steward, and so on down the line. In no case was the handwriting the same as that on the first slate. Could there be a stowaway on board? The ship was searched from stem to stern, but no stranger was found.

"Mr. Bruce," said the mystified captain, "what do you make of all this?"

Bruce had no theories. He was positive he had seen the man, and, of course, there was the writing on the slate.

The captain was not a superstitious man, but he had a feeling he should follow the command on the slateboard and see what happened. He gave orders to change the course of the vessel from southwest to northwest.

The apparition was seen at noon. Several hours later, the lookout reported an iceberg ahead. As the ship drew nearer, the crew saw an icebound vessel, damaged beyond repair, and on it many persons were waving and shouting at them. The wrecked ship, bound for Quebec, had been locked in the ice for several weeks and food supplies were about gone. The captain ordered boats lowered into the sea to bring back the hungry crew and passengers.

As the first mate was watching the rescued travellers climb aboard the ship, he gave a start and stared hard at one of them—a man who looked exactly like the stranger he had seen in the captain's cabin. The face was the same, the clothes were the same. The man, however, did not appear to recognize Mr. Bruce.

When all the passengers were aboard and were resting comfortably, Bruce said to his captain, "It was not a ghost I saw today, sir. The man's alive. I would swear in a courtroom it is the same man."

The captain, accompanied by the first mate, found the man talking with the captain of the icebound vessel and invited them into his cabin. Here he handed the stranger a slateboard and asked him to write a few words.

"What should I write, sir?" asked the puzzled man.

"Steer to the northwest."

The stranger did so, and the captain turned the slate over. The writing on the other side was a perfect match.

"The handwriting is the same," said the bewildered man. "But I only wrote one of these. Who wrote the other?"

Bruce explained that he had seen the double of the man writing on the slate about noon that day.

"Noon, eh?" said the other captain, who had been a silent spectator. "I recall that about that time this gentleman fell into a heavy sleep. After an hour he woke up and said, 'Captain, we shall be saved this very day.' He said he dreamed being on board a bark, and that she was coming to our rescue. He described her appearance and rig, and when we saw your vessel, she corresponded exactly to his description of her."

The stranger did not recall writing on the slate in his dream. All he remembered was getting the impression that the bark he saw would come to the rescue of his ship. However, he added, "Everything here on board seems to me quite familiar, yet I am sure I was never in your vessel before."

There is nothing fanciful about this story. Robert Dale Owen, a member of Congress and minister to Naples in the 19th century, wrote about it in 1859 in his *Footfalls on the Boundary of Another World.* Owen got the story from Captain J. S. Clarke of the schooner *Julia Hallock,* who first heard it from Robert Bruce himself. Captain Clarke described Bruce as "as truthful and straightforward a man as I ever met in my life. I stake my life upon it that he told me no lie."

THE "HEAD"
OF THE HOUSE

Ghosts have been seen and heard all over the world by all kinds of people—illiterate peasants, sophisticated city dwellers, hard-headed businessmen, poets, philosophers, even professors. Scientists have seen ghosts, but most of them are reluctant to talk about it for fear of ridicule by their colleagues. A friend of mine who is a physicist told me about an experience with perhaps the most unusual ghost in this book, but asked me not to use his real name.

Dr. Harvey Jordan is a shy, soft-spoken man of forty-five who enjoys the company of people but is more at home in his laboratory. While attending a conference on nuclear physics in Washington, D.C., a few years ago, he was invited to visit a young lady whose name had been given him by a mutual friend. Maria, a Jamaican girl of about twenty-eight, lived in a third-floor apartment in an old section of town. After climbing three rickety flights of stairs, Dr. Jordan rang the bell, wondering what his companion for the evening would be like.

He heard a light, musical voice call "Come in!" and he opened the door and walked down a very long, narrow hall to a livingroom. Maria was a lively girl, very attractive, and she immediately took his hand, led him to a chair, and offered him a drink of rum. Dr. Jordan, a non-drinker, refused the rum but Maria didn't mind. She loved to dance, and if Harvey would take her dancing, it would be heavenly.

They spent several hours in a nightclub dancing to the music of a small combo from Barbados. Dr. Jordan was not an especially good dancer, but he enjoyed having this vivacious young woman wheel him around the floor to exciting Latin-American rhythms. About midnight they took a cab back to her apartment, and Dr. Jordan was pleased when she asked him to come in. She put her key in the lock and opened the door.

Something was wrong. The room at the end of the hall was lighted, and he remembered she had turned off the light when they left.

"Who's there?" she said sharply. There was no answer.

"Who is there?" Silence.

Without waiting for Harvey, Maria ran down the hall while Dr. Jordan hung back, not knowing what to do. He was a scholar, not a man of action, and he had no wish to meet a burglar. Suddenly he heard Maria's voice from the living room. She sounded relieved.

"It's all right," she called. "It's only my husband."

Harvey felt even less inclined than before to join her. Maria had not told him she was married. His first impulse was to make an excuse and go home. Maria appeared at the end of the hall.

"It's all right, Harvey," she insisted. "It's only my husband. Come on in."

Hesitantly Dr. Jordan walked down the long hall, regretting that he was not back at his hotel and in bed, ready for another day's work at the conference. Finally, with leaden legs, he entered the living room.

"Harvey," said Maria, "I want you to meet my husband. This is Dr. Jordan," she said, turning to the table in the middle of the room.

Sitting on the table was a head. Just a head, no torso, no legs, no arms. But a *live* head, with its eyes fixed coldly on Dr. Jordan.

"How—do—you—do?" gulped the scientist. The head said nothing, continued to stare at him. It was lifelike, he thought, but certainly it couldn't be alive. Heads don't live without their bodies. The skull and face were rigid, immobile, but the eyes seemed alert.

"Come on, let's dance," said Maria.

Harvey wasn't sure whether she was talking to him or the head, but while she put on a record, he stared uncomfortably at the head, not daring to look away, while the eyes stared back, unblinking.

The music came on with a bang, and Maria grabbed Harvey and propelled him vigorously around the room.

"Why, Harvey," she said, "you're perspiring. What are you nervous about?"

Dr. Jordan muttered a non sequitur, something about it being late and that he had to get up early to attend the conference, but she ignored his remark, nestling close to him and singing along with the music.

As Maria bounced around the room with Harvey, he stole a glance at the head, and his blood congealed. *The eyes were moving*—following him—back and forth, back and forth. The head must be alive, thought Harvey with an inward groan, or perhaps it was the ghost of a head, the head of Maria's dead, not live, husband. Chills ran up Harvey's back. What punishment did the head have in store for him because he dared to go out with its wife?

"You're too stiff, honey," said Maria. "Let yourself go. Are you sure you don't want a drink?"

"No, no," Harvey mumbled. "I'm all right."

And as he danced, a strange thing happened. He

began to relax. The eyes that followed him to and fro were *kind* eyes. He was merely being observed in a friendly, interested way. The head had no evil intentions toward him. If it could speak, Harvey was certain, it would talk softly and reassuringly.

"I'll get you something out of the refrigerator," said Maria. "You're kind of jumpy—I don't know why."

She released Harvey and ran out to the kitchen. Dr. Jordan now could not take his eyes off the head, and the head looked steadily at him. Harvey smiled. He was sure the head smiled back.

When Dr. Jordan left Maria's apartment that night, he was completely relaxed. After an hour or two he regarded the head as an old friend, even though no words had been spoken.

Incredible? The story is written down just as it was told to me by a man whose integrity is unquestioned and who is highly regarded as an experimental physicist. He has done important research and has written several monographs based on his laboratory work. He is well-versed in the scientific method.

Dr. Jordan swears he had no drinks that night and that he has never suffered from hallucinations. However, although the "head" of the house appeared to be friendly, Harvey didn't see Maria again. He had no desire to meet other members of her family.

AN ODD COUPLE
OF GHOSTS

When ghostologists probe deeply enough, they can generally find out why a particular ghost acts the way he does. Sometimes an immediate contact is set up between ghost and mortal, and they are able to exchange information through sensory channels such as the voice and ear. Often a sensitive living person will pick up the thoughts of the ghost. Classic orthodox procedure has been to hold a séance, using the services of a medium, or to call in a member of the clergy, who seem to have influence over spirits. After he learns what the trouble is, the clergyman practices what may be called "ghost-therapy," and the ghost finally leaves whatever house he has been haunting, in better shape to handle the problems of the next world.

There are some ghost mysteries, however, which have never been solved, and one can only speculate what is behind the ghost's behavior. Dr. Harvey Jordan, who saw the friendly head on the living room table, told me about an encounter with the oddest pair of ghosts one could imagine together. As a team they have been haunting an old farmhouse for some two hundred years, meeting each night to carry out a project hardly appropriate to the station in life of either one. Dr. Jordan never found out what they were after, and it must rank among the leading ghost mysteries. Here is the story:

When Dr. Jordan was a very young man studying physics at an eastern university, he took a trip to France one summer and got a job as a construction foreman on a building project in the town of St. Quentin. There was a shortage of rooms at the time, and he was directed to a family on the outskirts of town. The French family had no room in their cottage, but they owned an abandoned farmhouse across the road, and they offered to fix it up as a temporary dwelling for him. Having no alternative, Dr. Jordan agreed.

The farmhouse was two hundred years old and in an advanced state of disrepair. It had a very large room, fifty feet in length, and a bed was put in at one end for Harvey's use. The "bedroom" walls were four feet thick throughout, but there were gaping holes along one wall that were almost round, with jagged edges. Harvey was not overjoyed at the thought of sleeping in this room, but as it was summer, the holes might admit some welcome breezes.

Although Harvey felt a sense of loneliness that first night in the old farmhouse, he was very tired after working all day with the construction crew and fell into a deep sleep. During the night he was awakened by the noise of a blunt instrument thumping rhythmically against the bedroom wall. He sat up and listened, but the noise stopped and he went back to sleep.

About half an hour later he was awakened again by what sounded like a battering ram being driven against the side of the building. The sound seemed to come from the other end of the room. Harvey stood up sleepily, put on his bathrobe, and walked the length of the room—fifty feet. With each step the hammering grew louder. When he reached the source of the noise, he peered through a small hole in the wall about half a foot in diameter.

Two figures were pounding a long, thick metal object against the wall. The taller figure, holding the front end of the object, was dressed like a priest. Just behind him, his small hands cupped under the rear end of the instrument, was a dwarflike form.,

"Say, what's going on—" but before Harvey could finish his question, the metal object came toward him and hit the wall. Fragments of rock flew in all directions, some of them stinging his face, while the larger pieces fell on the floor. He spoke again, this time from a bit farther back, but they paid no attention to him as they kept hammering out the opening in the wall.

It was a strange, eerie sight—the priest and the dwarf methodically pounding the solid wall, ignoring Dr. Jordan's presence. Then they vanished—priest, dwarf, and metal instrument.

Somewhat shaken, Dr. Jordan walked back to his bed, but now he was unable to sleep. When he finally dozed off, he was awakened again by the sound of rocks clattering to the floor of the room. "Here, you'll have to stop that!" he called out in English and then in halting French, but the hammering continued.

In the morning he examined the hole. It was much larger than it had been when he had gone to sleep—almost circular in shape.

At first Harvey said nothing to the family in the

cottage. Each night he was jarred out of sleep several times by the hammering, and often he would walk over to where a new hole was being hollowed out and make a feeble protest. So far as the priest and the dwarf were concerned, however, he just wasn't there. And then, suddenly, they weren't there.

As the weeks went by, more holes were hollowed out, and each night the hammering was nearer his bed. At the end of his two months' stay, there were many breezes cooling Harvey as he slept.

Finally he told the family in the cottage.

"Oh, don't mind them," said the peasant wife. "That's only the Father and the little fellow who is helping him. They've been working on the farmhouse for two hundred years. They won't bother you."

Who were they and why were they systematically taking the farmhouse apart? And why a priest and a dwarf? In answer the peasant lady merely shrugged. She didn't know what they were doing, and it made no difference to her.

No one else in town could explain what was going on nor did they care to find out. The townspeople felt that if two such unlikely ghosts as a priest and a dwarf wanted to hammer for two hundred years on the four-feet-thick walls of a farmhouse, that was their own business.

THE GHOST WHO KEPT PEEKING

Another mystery ghost was seen in 1881 by several members of an English family and was investigated by the British Society for Psychical Research. This ghost had the disconcerting habit of peeking around corners at the women of the house, but since he did so only when they were properly dressed, he couldn't be classed as a voyeur-type ghost. It was discovered later that he was looking for something in the house, but no one ever found out what it was.

The peeking ghost first appeared three weeks after the family rented a remote villa. One morning, while the mother was playing the piano in the drawing room, she looked over her shoulder and saw the ghost peering at her from around the corner of a folding door. She saw only the upper half of his body and described him later as a tall man with dark hair parted in the middle, a mustache, and a very doleful expression on his face. When she went over to get a closer look, he disappeared.

The following August she saw him in the drawing room again, peeking through the bay window. Two weeks later she was playing cricket in the garden with her two young boys when the face appeared again, this time peeking around the kitchen door. She threw down her bat and ran in, but the face vanished.

Her stepdaughter, not knowing about her mother's experiences, also saw the peeking ghost. She, too, was playing the piano when the man's head and shoulders emerged shyly from behind the folding door. She gave a similar description of the ghost—dark hair parted in the middle and a melancholy expression.

A few weeks later the stepdaughter was alone one evening in the dining room, playing bezique, when the ghost peeked at her again. Then she went upstairs and, in her own words, "I was playing battledore and shuttlecock with my oldest brother in his bedroom. I looked sideways, over my shoulder, in order to strike the shuttlecock, and saw the face on the landing." Her brother saw the ghost, too, and called out, "There's a man on the landing."

Up to this point, one might surmise that the ghost liked music and games, since he always seemed to do his peeking when the ladies were playing the piano or indulging in some girlish sport such as bezique, shuttlecock, battledore, or cricket. But later that year the peeking ghost finally gave a hint as to his real motive.

The mother was walking down the stairs one evening when she heard a voice coming from the direction of her two sons' bedroom. The voice was saying in very sad, low tones, "I can't find it. I can't find it." When she entered the room, the boys were fast asleep and no one else was there. Her stepdaughter, who was in the living room, also heard the voice and called up, "What are you looking for?" Since the father was out for the evening and the servants were in the kitchen, it was very much a ghostly voice.

What was the peeking ghost looking for? A spirit carries into the next world much unfinished business that will not let him rest until it has been disposed of. Dr. Jordan's odd couple of ghosts were not going to stop until they had completely demolished the old farmhouse. The peeking ghost seemed determined to go on searching indefinitely for whatever he had lost in the villa.

A LAST
HIGH NOTE

Many ghosts talk, whisper, laugh, chuckle, giggle, sigh, and sing. Perhaps the last ghosts I should write about are those who hit the highest notes of all—they whistle. In the Gilbert Islands, these whistlers are called *Taani-kani-momoi* and are the ghosts of the newly dead, who fly over the islands like scouts and take note of what is happening. Then they whistle the news to the natives.

Sir Arthur Grimble, in his book *We Chose The Islands*, tells about an encounter with these friendly whistling spirits. While consulting an island psychic for news of a friend, he heard a single note, then little excited whistles like birdcalls. The psychic, interpreting the sounds, said the spirits had informed her that his friend was dead. They also told her that a Japanese ship he was awaiting would return to the island in exactly twenty-three days. Both news items proved accurate.

POSTSCRIPT

The defense rests. This book started out to prove that most ghosts are kindly, friendly, affectionate, and fun-loving. A few of them play rough at times, but on the whole they want to enjoy the company of mortals and help out when they are needed. Often the friendly ghost needs help himself but cannot get through the psychic barrier. At such times you must try to understand and assist your ghost.

Not every true ghost story goes into the record. Because ghosts have been cruelly maligned and their motives misinterpreted, people in general don't like to meet them, and when they do, they keep silent about it. In addition to those stories that have been investigated and authenticated, there must be countless ghosts who came and went and were either ignored or frightened back into their spirit world. These ghosts have never been discussed or written about, yet they deserve thoughtful consideration.

Ghosts are not only friendly, they are infinitely interesting. Reader, if you should meet a ghost, don't turn tail and run. Be sympathetic, speak to him (or her), offer him a cup of coffee or a drink. Chances are he has an absorbing tale for you to hear. Listen to him.

And pass his story on to me, won't you? Having had a taste of friendly ghosts, I can't seem to get enough of them. I'll be waiting to hear from you.

H.B.G.